Mansfield *c.*1913
North & West

500m

MANSFIELD
A Pictorial History

To Jim
Best wishes
from Roy - Sylvia
Christmas - 05.

WELCOME TO MANSFIELD

19 December 1896. Despite freezing temperatures, Mansfield celebrates its first ceremonial royal visit for several hundred years, as the Duke and Duchess of York arrive from an overnight stop at Welbeck Abbey. As King George V and Queen Mary, they would return to the town twice, in 1914 and 1928.

MANSFIELD
A Pictorial History

David J. Bradbury

Phillimore

2005

Published by
PHILLIMORE & CO. LTD,
Shopwyke Manor Barn, Chichester, West Sussex, England

ISBN 1 86077 337 0

Printed and bound in Great Britain by
CAMBRIDGE PRINTING

This book is dedicated to Albert Sorby Buxton (1867-1932)
Mansfield's best historian and best artist,
and an enthusiastic photographer too.

List of Illustrations

Frontispiece: Royal visitors, December 1806

Acknowledgements

The pictures in this book have been obtained from the following sources: Mansfield Central Library, frontispiece, 11, 16, 23, 26, 29, 34, 51, 57, 58, 63, 65, 66, 99, 102, 111-7, 136, 148, 149, 151-4, 156, 157, 159, 160; Nottingham Central Library (County Local Studies Library), 1, 47-9, 68, 101, 120; Nottinghamshire Archives, 12, 93; Author, 25, 59, 108.

Also, for convenience, I have used the Old Mansfield Society's negative of the painting in picture 14.

All other pictures are taken from the collections of Mansfield Museum. The largest single source is the museum's collection of glass-plate negatives taken by A.S. Buxton between about 1895 and 1925. Because the museum devotes almost half its space to a varied programme of temporary exhibitions (in an environment very different from the regimented cabinets of picture 133) and because many items would be damaged by long-term exposure to light, much of its collection is usually kept in storage. Given notice by phone or letter, however, the museum can produce any item from its stores, or give access to collections for research purposes.

Most of Mr Buxton's historical paintings are on permanent display, as are many other items of local interest. In addition to local history material, the museum retains in storage a large portion of its old natural history collections, plus an assortment of household items from the past, many of which can be borrowed by schools.

Further details are obtainable from local Tourist Information Centres, or by writing to The Curator, Mansfield Museum and Art Gallery, Leeming Street, Mansfield, Nottinghamshire NG18 1NG.

And finally: this book, like numerous others, could not have been produced without the help and encouragement of Sonia Gill.

Introduction

It may be a cliché to say that Mansfield's origins are lost in the mists of time, but it is absolutely true, more so than for most other towns of comparable importance. Mansfield lies at a junction of ancient routes, and there are remains of Romano-British farms in the vicinity, but archaeology has, so far, totally failed to reveal any firm evidence about the early development of the settlement.

Mansfield simply appears, in Domesday Book of 1086, as one of the most important administrative centres in Nottinghamshire, controlling a great swathe of crown estates across the north of the county. It is recorded that the tenant of one of these holdings had the job of shoeing the king's horse when he visited Mansfield, and government accounts from just a couple of generations after Domesday refer to the king's residence there. But we can only speculate as to the purpose of the royal interest, and even the location of the residence is unknown. Though the hunting in Sherwood may have enticed the Saxon kings as it did their Norman successors, the subsidiary estates could have had a less frivolous purpose. They form a wide band, following the valleys of four rivers which cross the main north-south routes through the county, and it is possible that they were intended not only to furnish provisions for royal visitors, but also to provide a permanent, self-sustaining defensive force, ready to do battle at the river-crossings against invaders from the north.

For centuries, since the Romans had failed to conquer northern Europe, trouble had often visited Britain from the north. Until about half a century before the Norman Conquest, England effectively ended at the Humber. The north-east Midlands formed a buffer zone between north and south, absorbing new populations as successive generations of northern invaders conquered the area and then came to terms with the southern English. In the 10th century, the territories attached to Nottingham, Derby, Lincoln, Stamford and Leicester formed a semi-independent confederation called 'The Five Boroughs', home to an ethnic mix of English, Danes and a few communities of Norse settlers. Though this little nation did not survive very long, its spirit still sets the area apart from the rest of the Midlands.

Though Mansfield's part in the history of the years before 1086 remains a matter of conjecture, the influence of the times on the town is clear. Even the local placenames have a cosmopolitan flavour: the river Maun, and Mansfield itself, seem to take their names from the ancient Celtic *mam*, a breast (as in Derbyshire's 'Mam Tor'), referring perhaps to the gently rounded Hamilton Hill near the river's source. The 'field' part of the town's name, though, is Old English and indicates a large area of open land (also nearby on this edge of Sherwood Forest are Ashfield and Hatfield). Then again, most of the local names of fields and streets are of Danish origin: West Gate and Ratcliffe Gate, for example, do not refer to gateways, but to the Danish word for a street or major road.

As for the information actually given in Domesday Book, the compilers were so confused by the huge list of places controlled from Mansfield that the information on the town itself is less than for some nearby villages. Mansfield's statistics are combined with those for Sutton in Ashfield and Skegby, which were attached to the town to provide supplies for royal visitors. Between these three places there were five freeholders, 35 tenant farmers, 20 tenant smallholders, two churches, two priests, one watermill and one fish-farm (plus a very large area of woodland). All we can say for certain is that the total number of householders was barely the equal of some single villages elsewhere in the county – had many tenants been killed in battle against the Normans?

Mansfield's status quickly declined under the new regime, but it long remained a crown estate, with outliers as far afield as Scofton near Worksop. Sometimes this valuable property would be given into the custody of favoured barons, such as the Earls of Chester, but for much of the time it was administered by the locals themselves. During one such period, in 1227, the townsfolk were granted a charter for a market to be held every Monday. This turned out to be a mistake for Henry III, as his great lords were not keen to take custody of a town where the citizens had such independent privileges. When the heiress of the Earl of Chester was granted the property a few years later, the locals were persuaded to give up their charter. Later records show that the Lord's market was subsequently held every Thursday.

For convenience, this was also the day of the manor court, which governed the day-to-day functioning of Mansfield and its dependencies. Most importantly, as land ownership was by the copyhold system, the court records served as a central register of property, with individuals holding copies of the entries relating to their own land and houses. Most of the early court records seem to have been lost centuries ago, probably destroyed by fire, but a few odd samples do survive. Notable is a long roll of parchment containing the court records for 1315-16, which include the year's estate transfers, plus a wide variety of other cases, showing how the court held the community together, dealing with disputes between neighbours, petty crime and anti-social behaviour.

A few years older are a list of copyholders made in 1292-3 and a full statement of the rules by which the court operated, made about the same time. This landholders' list and tax records from a few years later show the different social mixes in Mansfield and its neighbouring communities. While Sutton in Ashfield was dominated by a small number of prosperous farmers, and Mansfield Woodhouse had an extraordinary number of independent but poor smallholders (more copyholders in total than the parent town), Mansfield itself was a prosperous trading centre supporting a variety of occupations such as smith, tailor and weaver. Even the beginnings of the town's industrial prosperity were evident, with the presence of a fulling mill for preparing woollen cloth. Sherwood Forest had become a centre for sheep farming, largely controlled by the various local monasteries, so while Newark became wealthy as an export centre, Mansfield had turned to the manufacturing side of the business. As well as the fulling mill, a large area of windswept land on the south-west side of the town had been set aside as a tenter ground, where treated cloth was stretched out on tenterhooks to dry. Even at the end of the 17th century, long after the monasteries had been closed down, traveller Celia Fiennes observed that Mansfield was a centre for the making of 'tammy' cloth, a very high-quality woollen fabric.

To the Crown, however, the main function of the town was its rôle as administrative centre for Sherwood Forest. Records survive of great courts held here in the 13th and 14th centuries, dealing with offences as serious as organised poaching, trivial as the taking of branches for firewood (not so much an offence as a perk of living in the Forest, and only a small fine was payable). Many important local men augmented their incomes by working as Forest officials.

From about 1500, the manor court rolls form an almost continuous sequence, but they include only the property business. These transactions tell us a great deal about the geography of Mansfield, and about the pattern of property ownership. However, only the area within two or three kilometres of the town and its various outliers was held as copyhold farmland. Beyond this was the open Forest, used mostly for pasture. It was not necessarily heavily wooded; for example the word 'storth', as in Dalestorth, indicates an area of brushwood, lacking really large trees. Much of this Forest land was quite suitable for cultivation though, and over the centuries, with permission from the Forest authorities, many areas were fenced off and converted to farmland. One relic of this process until recent years was the 'Eight Men's Intake', an area of Forest land off Sutton Road, acquired for the parish in the Middle Ages and run by eight trustees.

The core of copyhold land was originally divided into three great open fields (North, West and South) in which local farmers each held a number of strips for ploughing. Early in the 16th century, families like the Dands began to acquire strips next to each other, and to surround them with fences and hedges to form 'closes'. These small fields could now be used for a variety of purposes: growing crops, grazing livestock or even, as with the Dands, quarrying the fine building stone underneath.

Quarrying had been another early Mansfield industry, but it had been run by the Crown and the Church for their own purposes such as improvements to Nottingham Castle and the building of Southwell Minster. The town itself was largely built of timber. The Dands' move into this field (to be precise, a close within the old North Field!) came at a convenient time; there had been two major fires in Mansfield in the 16th century, each of which destroyed dozens of houses. From this time onwards even the old timber houses began to acquire stone cladding, and the appearance of the whole town was gradually transformed.

The Mansfield of 1600, however, had much in common with the Mansfield of 1300. It was still a market town (and in the 14th century had been awarded a charter for a fair on 29 June, the day of its patron saints, Peter and Paul). The wool and weaving trades still prospered, and the local upper crust still worked as Forest officers. Though there is no evidence that Queen Elizabeth enjoyed hunting (in fact the royal hunting lodge at Clipstone had been disused for a century or more) the timber from Sherwood Forest was still a crucial national resource, for repairs to official buildings, and for making the warships on which the country had depended so much during the queen's long reign.

Before considering the events of the 17th century, which had many effects on the town, I shall explore the earlier development of some notable Mansfield institutions.

We have already seen the church referred to in Domesday Book, the earliest record of the town. Some stonework at the base of the tower of St Peter's Church dates from about this time, but, like most parish churches, it is a patchwork of extensions and improvements made over many centuries. Soon after Domesday, the churches and chapels in Mansfield and its dependent estates were given to Lincoln Minster (originally to the Bishop, but later transferred to the Dean). In the town itself, the Dean of Lincoln became lord of a little manor; though its buildings and land were intermingled with the Crown holdings, the inhabitants were subject to the Dean's jurisdiction.

Though St Peter's Church remained the only one in the town until quite recently, it was not the only religious institution to own property here. The practice of endowing 'chantry priests' to say prayers for your family was very common among the well-to-do in the Middle Ages, and by the late 14th century Southwell Minster had 10 such priests. They were beneficiaries of a most generous gift, including property in a number of communities throughout the county. Some of this was at Mansfield, including a residence on Church Street, almost opposite the church, which logically enough came to be called the 'Ten Chantry Priests' House'. Town records indicate other properties held by other churches, and St Peter's itself frequently received gifts of money and property. Under the copyhold system, however, it was difficult to give land in perpetuity, so many chantries died out when the term of their property ownership expired. For example, in 1290, there were altars at Mansfield dedicated to the Virgins Mary and Catherine, and Saints William and Margaret, but these soon ceased to be maintained.

The last chantry in Mansfield was probably that established in 1515 by Cicily Flogan, widow of Robert Flogan, a local businessman. She was landlady of the *Hart Inn* on Church Street (later the *White Hart*) and she gave that, with its farmland and other properties, for 99 years to fund a chantry. She appointed John Porter as priest, to be paid eight marks (£5) per year. As it happened, this was a mistake, for the amount to be paid was not far short of the entire rental from the properties, leaving almost nothing for administration and maintenance. After a while, the buildings became so ruinous that the trustees appointed in Cicily's will had to step in and reduce the amount paid to Porter while repairs were undertaken. This was just the first of many troubles to beset the Flogan chantry, the next being the Chantry Act of 1547, which diverted the resources of the chantries to more 'practical' good works. It may have been this legislation which prompted Oliver Dand in 1552 to make his own pious gift, of a cottage by the churchyard which was to be used for a high school (*gymnasio*) and elementary school. Under the 1547 Act, the income from Flogan's chantry and the Ten Chantry Priests' estate in Mansfield had been awarded to St Peter's, and it seems likely that the 'unlerned' Porter (who had been allowed to retain his position at a slightly reduced salary) became the first master of what was now effectively a church school.

Under the Catholic Queen Mary there was nearly a return to the old ways, but Queen Elizabeth, responding to a petition from the inhabitants of the town, established a secure legal position for the school by granting letters patent in 1561 for the establishment of a Free Grammar School, with a master and assistant. Despite all these gifts and privileges, in 1564 there was another crisis for the Flogan chantry endowment, as two of her relatives stepped forward to claim the estates. However, the 99-year term was still unexpired, and after a battle in the Court of Chancery (during which some very strange things happened to the relevant court rolls) the claimants were persuaded to release the estate to the Grammar School governors.

Under the original arrangement, the governors were the vicar and churchwardens, who administered the former chantry endowments with those of the church (supervised by eight 'assistants' chosen by the parishioners). This joint administration would lead to a lot of trouble in later years – but there is much to tell first about the greater troubles of the 17th century.

It began badly. As part of its never-ending quest for extra cash, the government proposed selling off the royal manor, which would deprive the townsfolk of many privileges. Though a petition, with detailed arguments against the sale, was raised in 1602, the manor of Mansfield ultimately passed into the hands of the Earl of

Shrewsbury. This sale did not include the Forest area, but a few years later King James offered the freehold of the cultivated 'Intake' lands (reserving a very small annual rent). The 'Eight Men's Intake' was bought by two London agents in 1607, and subsequently sold by them to the eight trustees for £20.

The family of Gilbert, Earl of Shrewsbury, held the manor of Mansfield for nearly thirty years, but during the 1630s they first leased it, then sold it outright to William Cavendish, Earl of Newcastle. Cavendish, whose main residence was Welbeck Abbey, was a Royalist and was forced into exile during the Civil War, all his estates being placed under the control of agents. He had probably had little control over the people of Mansfield anyway. There is no sign that the town felt obliged to support one side or the other, though the numerous wealthy gentlemen who found Mansfield a congenial place to live certainly made their individual choices, often dragging their tenants with them to battle. There were no battles near the town, though armies would march through along the main roads from time to time.

The Restoration of the Monarchy in 1660 brought mixed blessings. William Cavendish, promoted to Duke of Newcastle, was able to reclaim his estates (minus most of the valuable timber, which had been stripped during the war). Then the government, still short of money, decided to sell off much of the remaining Forest land, so Cavendish bought as much as he could within 'his' part of Sherwood. It was this deal which made him not just lord of the manor, but the largest landowner in Mansfield, holding a great crescent of potential farmland beyond the ancient town fields.

Not all the timber was gone from Sherwood Forest, and Cavendish now owned much of what remained. The iron industry, which had been active along the Derbyshire border for centuries, was just learning how to produce metal in large quantities, and needed massive amounts of fuel, so canny Cavendish offered timber rights on many of his local estates, including Mansfield, to a consortium of ironworkers. As in the Amazon rainforest today, industrialists destroyed the woodland, ignoring the old policies of replanting, and then farmers moved in.

Mansfield prospered in these days; still a major market town, it was also home to healthy textile, leather and malt industries (the former boosted by use of the mechanised 'knitting frame', particularly useful for making hosiery). The roads, and consequently the inns, remained busy; in 1675 there were over 40 licensed victuallers. Like most of the country, this town suffered occasionally from epidemics (in 1631, the market had had to close for two months, so serious was the risk of infection), but history records no great catastrophes. As in the Civil War, the most notable thing about Mansfield was an odd mixture of prosperity and unimportance.

This was due partly to the attitude of the Cavendish family, which seems to have been persuaded to leave the townspeople to run their own affairs as they had under Crown control. Perhaps more important, however, was Mansfield's lack of official status. This was illustrated most clearly by the Five Mile Act of 1665, part of the government's attempt to dampen down the religious strife between the established Anglican Church and the Puritans, who had been dominant under Cromwellian rule before 1660. Under this law, preachers who refused to conform were prohibited from living within five miles of any place where they used to preach before 1660, or any place with borough or city status.

Because Mansfield, though a large town with many wealthy inhabitants, was not then a borough, numerous nonconformist preachers came to live here, creating the nucleus of a strong Presbyterian religious tradition. The 'official' Anglican priest at that time, John Firth, had served happily both before and after 1660, and made no serious attempts to interfere with his rivals. One group which did suffer more was the Society of Friends (the Quakers), which had numerous members in the town, thanks to the personal visits of founder George Fox in the 1640s. There were no Quaker preachers, but the emphasis on personal conscience meant that individual members were frequently picked upon by malicious local officials. A particular problem was the Quakers' natural unwillingness to pay tithes for the upkeep of the town's church; the job of tithe collection had been farmed out to private enterprise, and was performed with ruthless effectiveness.

Vicar Firth, of course, was probably in it for the money anyway. In his later years various unusual practices came to light, particularly regarding the way in which he used the church and Grammar School lands. He held the official seal for documents, and the eight supervising 'Assistants' had increasingly been kept ignorant of the way he and the churchwardens managed the estates (including the Eight Men's Intake). It had become effectively impossible to distinguish church from school income (partly because many old documents referred to payments for a 'preacher', meaning a chantry priest, forerunner of the schoolmaster, but easily interpreted as meaning the vicar) and in 1682 the schoolmaster, James Holcott, had to take the matter to the Court of Chancery. Firth persuaded the Assistants, and thus the court (but not the poor teachers) to agree on a division of £60 yearly income to the vicar, £30 to the school. This did not actually answer the original question, so in 1699 three local gentlemen took the ageing vicar to court again. This case revealed, among other matters, that Firth was finding all sorts of ways to increase his income, through 'fees', raised rents etc. But Firth died, so the problem was not solved, and the Court of Chancery would still be hearing arguments over 150 years later.

It may not be a coincidence that several people living in Mansfield at this time set up their own charities for educational purposes. One was Quaker widow Elizabeth Heath, who with her nephew supplied £100 in 1686 to help pay for a 'working school', where children could learn techniques of the textile industry, such as spinning and knitting. The appointed teacher took the money and ran, so in her will a few years later Elizabeth left her estate for the provision of almshouses instead of education. Samuel Brunts, who had inherited lands in Mansfield, Nottingham and elsewhere, died in 1711, having made a bequest in his will for educational purposes; Faith Clerkson did the same with her inheritance in 1725. These three charitable benefactors, like Cicily Flogan, are still gratefully remembered in Mansfield today.

Another century ended: the population had grown; the rich had perhaps become richer; a few isolated farms and houses had appeared on the former Forest land, and the Forest officials had little or nothing to do although of course they still collected their salaries. But Mansfield in 1700 was effectively a stone-built version of the town in 1300. Only the clatter of the knitting frames, and the work of the ironmasters at furnaces and forges a few miles away would have given a clue to the future.

For much of the 18th century, Mansfield continued to mark time. Bonnie Prince Charlie's advance to Derby in 1745 caused a brief panic, but was soon a matter for wry humour. From the 1750s, some of the all-important main roads began to be improved, thanks to the creation of privatised 'turnpike trusts', and fast coach services used the town as a handy stopping point. And then in 1771 Richard Arkwright moved from Nottingham to Cromford in Derbyshire, because he had found that his new cotton spinning machine could very effectively be used with water power.

The main purpose of this book is to show what happened in Mansfield after that moment: a continuing revolution and acceleration which hurled the town from its centuries of complacent comfort into the dizzying world we inhabit today. In these next few paragraphs, I would like to cut across the thematic divisions of the Pictorial History to suggest some general patterns.

Within 15 years of Arkwright's move, there were four or five water-powered spinning mills on the Maun in Mansfield. To make all the machinery, iron foundries were established, using sand quarried in the Berry Hill area to make the moulds. Communications were improved by building more turnpike roads, and in 1819 a crude railway was introduced, so that machinery (and the very effective moulding sand) could be exported while coal was brought in to fuel the foundries and the next development, steam-powered textile mills. Mansfield grew rapidly, not so much by increasing its area as by cramming tiny houses onto plots within the town (though the wealthy did have opulent houses built out beyond the town fringes). Political unrest among the growing population was met, in the British tradition, by general improvements to the quality of life; the town, which had been dirty and unwelcoming in 1800, was utterly transformed by 1840, thanks to simple improvements such as street-widening, gas street-lighting, proper drainage and house guttering, removal of obstacles to pedestrians etc. To deal with the unemployed, a large workhouse was built in 1837 to serve the whole district.

The influx of workers also changed other aspects of the town. In religion, the Presbyterians and Quakers were joined by Methodists, Baptists, Congregationalists and others. The demand for entertainment and escape forced the provision in the 1830s of many new public houses (carefully not licensed to sell spirits). New clubs and sports teams appeared (and often quickly disappeared) while spectacular travelling theatres visited the town each winter.

The lack of a steam railway nearly killed the town's industries, so a line to Nottingham was made in 1849, followed by others to Worksop and Southwell. Sure enough, this gave the town a boost, enabling much more effective distribution of products like foundry castings (including lamp-posts for the Embankment in London, and pillar-boxes) and building stone. Since 1849, the town has continued to experience booms and slumps. History suggests that the way out of the latter has always been to invest wisely, to make Mansfield fit for the future.

'Mansfield'

There's a bright little town,
That is very well known,
It stands very close to the Maun;
Should you find it your duty,
To look at its beauty,
You should rise at the early dawn.

Go up Berry Hill,
When 'tis calm and still,
And look down in the vale below;
'Tis a glorious sight,
As soon as it's light,
And will set your cheeks in a glow.

There's the best of stone,
And for this alone,
Mansfield will not be forgotten;
And there's plenty of lace,
In this sweet little place,
As well as very good cotton.

And there are charity schools,
With some excellent rules,
To keep the scholars in order;
And Thompson's name,
As well as his fame,
Will be sung beyond the border.

There are railway stations,
To suit your relations,
Whenever they come to take lunch;
And if you've a mind,
And feel so inclined,
You can treat them to a glass of punch.

There is plenty of coals,
That is dug out of holes,
From many large pits close by;
And a great deal of corn,
That is stored in the barn,
As well as some excellent rye.

We have a Town Hall,
But rather too small,
To accommodate all new comers;
When it was erected,
'Twas hardly expected,
We should want more builders & plumbers.

A monument rise,
Pointing to the skies,
It stands in the Market's centre;
This splendid design,
Was done by friend Hine,
'Tis seen when the market you enter.

And now for a word,
If you have not heard
Of the famous Mansfield bells;
Their sound is so clear,
When heard by the ear,
Over hills, and meadows and dells.

And what do you think,
Of the skating rink,
'Tis a place of resort well known,
Where the belles and beaus,
Glide well on their toes,
They seldom fall to the ground.

And in addition,
There's a commission,
Comprised of men that's well known,
Who will try to suit ye,
By doing their duty,
And gain the respect of the town.

Success to this town,
A place of renown,
May prosperity still be thine;
May the people act right,
And be always polite,
And for ever in history shine.

From *A Selection of Original Poetry* by William Sargent, stationer and tailor of Mansfield, 1879.

Religion

1 The Church of St Peter and St Paul, by the river, is by far the oldest religious institution in Mansfield. It was established in Saxon times, and the lower stages of the present tower, seen here c.1895, were built in the 12th century. The church had become so crowded by the 18th century that galleries had to be built inside.

2   The galleries were attached to the pillars of the nave, a precarious arrangement which was happily abandoned when the church was restored in 1871. Like most parish churches, St Peter's evolved over many centuries; for example the nave pillars probably date from 1300, while the east window contains stained glass of 1905 in a setting of 1475.

3   Thanks to the generosity of the late Henry Gally Knight, a local gentleman with an interest in church architecture, the overcrowding at St Peter's was solved in 1856, with the opening of St John's Church, designed by H.I. Stevens. In this view, c.1904, the church is flanked by the vicarage and the National School, built in 1861.

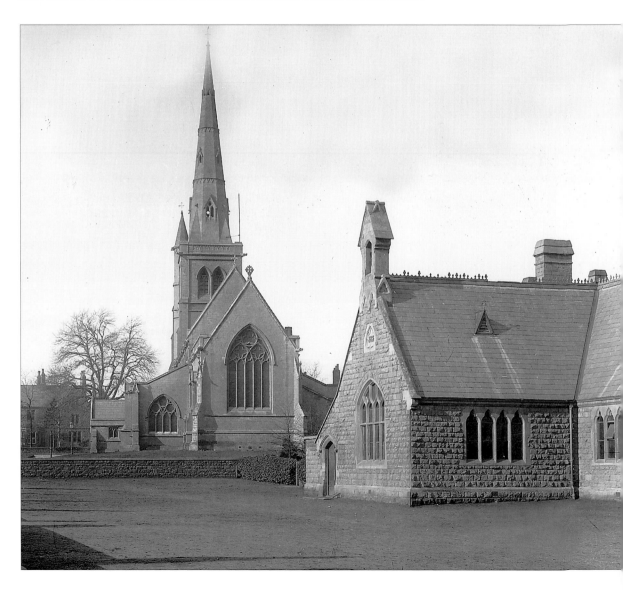

4 St John's is just a year older than the beautiful cemetery on Nottingham Road; like the church, St Peter's graveyard was also intolerably crowded. The building in this late Victorian view is the twin chapels, one side for Anglicans, the other for dissenters.

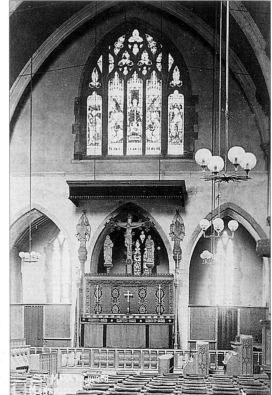

5 The pace of growth in Victorian Mansfield was so rapid that another church soon became necessary. St Mark's parish was established in 1889, but the permanent church was not opened until 1897. Though the exterior is surprisingly plain, the interior (pictured about 1905) is a classic of late Victorian design, by Temple Moore and associates.

6 Anglican church-building was not just a matter of keeping up with the population; the established Church also had to compete with other denominations. The town's second oldest place of worship is the Old Meeting House, built in 1702 off Stockwell Gate, originally Presbyterian but now Unitarian. This underexposed Buxton photograph of the choir about 1910 shows the Victorian porch, regrettably replaced since.

7 George Fox, founder of the Society of Friends, or Quakers, lived for a time near Mansfield, and he or the remarkable Elizabeth Hooton of Skegby probably converted Elizabeth Heath. The latter died in 1693 a wealthy widow, founding a charity to provide accommodation for elderly women, and also providing a graveyard for the Quakers. The picture shows her grave.

8　This, the town's first proper Methodist chapel, was built on Stockwell Gate in 1791. In 1797 the Methodists split, and the Wesleyan branch had to find new accommodation. In 1815, however, the chapel became vacant, and was bought by the Baptists. They in turn built a new chapel on Rosemary Street in 1912, having planned expansion for nearly forty years.

9 The Wesleyan Methodists bought Stanhope House on Bridge Street (see picture 107) in 1810, and soon rebuilt the central part as a chapel. That in turn was replaced by the present church in 1864. Since this photograph was taken, about 1905, there have been further changes, such as the removal of the organ to the rear gallery.

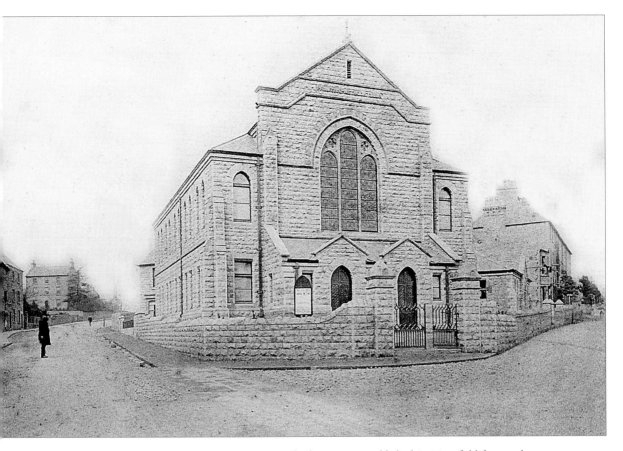

10   Another branch of Wesley's stock, the Primitive Methodists, were established in Mansfield for nearly seventy years before they managed to build this large chapel at the end of Leeming Street (which remains in religious use at the time of writing). This photograph may well have been taken in 1887 – the year the building was completed.

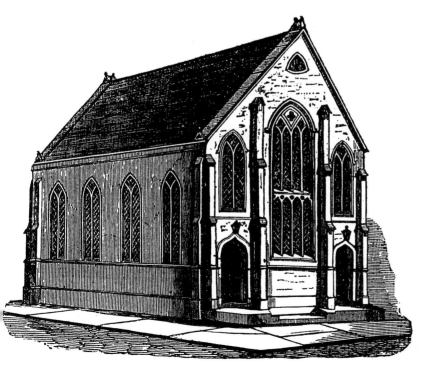

11   This building also survived into the 21st century, though few could guess where. The Railway Side chapel of the United Methodists, on Clerkson Street (pictured here in 1871) was later extended and converted with a fake half-timbered effect. Their current Nottingham Road church was built in 1913.

CONGREGATIONAL CHURCH

Fothergill Watson
Architect
Nottingham

9 March 1877

Scale 8 Feet to an Inch

Elevation Towards Wood Street

12 The Congregationalists built Mansfield's showiest Victorian chapel in 1878, replacing a plain building off Stockwell Gate, thanks to the designs of Fothergill Watson, who had been born in Mansfield in 1841, and became a successful architect in Nottingham (later swopping his surname and forename).

13 Here is Watson's building at the top of West Gate, just before the First World War, surprisingly complemented by a cast-iron urinal. Sadly, both have since been demolished, as has the equally attractive lamp-post. Nationally, the Congregationalists now form part of the United Reformed Church, but they had too few followers in Mansfield to build a new chapel.

Industry

14 Until recently, there were several quarries around Mansfield, producing different tints of high-quality 'freestone' for building, plus the famous foundry moulding sand. This 1857 picture by J. Isherwood, of the Maun near Quarry Lane, shows how nature turned former quarry areas into beauty spots.

15 There has been a textile industry in Mansfield since the Middle Ages, and the town was one of the first to benefit from the invention of water-powered spinning and knitting machines. Bath Mill (pictured here by A.A. Richardson) was founded in 1792 to spin wool by water power, but soon acquired a steam engine, and later became a hosiery mill.

16　The Old Town Mill was converted from corn grinding to cotton spinning in 1784. The dominant feature of this remarkable panorama is its young brother, the New Town Mill, under construction in 1870 to the right of the gas works. The remarkable thing about the panorama is, of course, not the smoggy haze, but the lack of a viaduct!

17　Most of the town's early textile mills used the power of the River Maun, but the Reed Mills at Bleak Hills, built in 1795 as an extension of the Stanton family's business (and seen here about 1920 in a painting by W. Daws), were on the tributary Coldwell Brook, with an unusually large mill-pond to ensure a steady flow.

18　Mansfield's first water-powered textile mill was already working on or near this site by Bath Lane in the 13th century. It was then a fulling mill, for treating the woollen cloth made in the town, but in the late 18th century the Stanton family built a cotton mill. The enlarged mill became a shoe factory in the 1890s, and still stands in 2005.

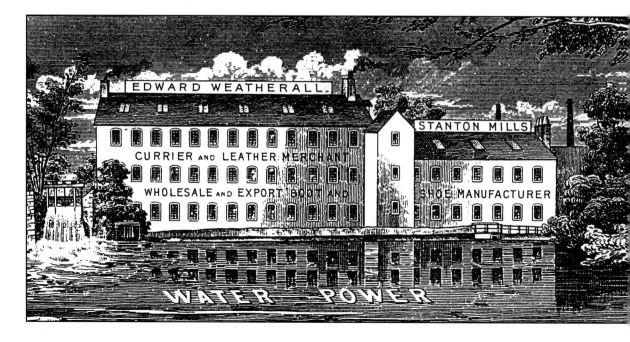

19 In fact, the leather trade in Mansfield also dates back to the Middle Ages. The unusual shutters and washable paving seen in this alley leading down to St Peter's Church are clues that here, in the heart of the town, is one of the most unpleasant, smelly industrial sites imaginable – a tannery, in use until Victorian times.

20 Though the tanneries were sited by streams (the Maun and the Lady Brook) to give a constant water supply, most of the shoemakers lived along Stockwell Gate, so it was natural that George Royce and James Gascoine should establish the business which became the Mansfield Shoe Company there in the late 1860s (see also picture 37).

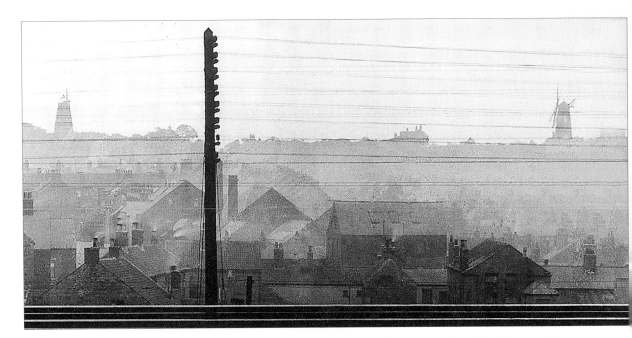

21 When the textile industry took over the best water-power sites in the 1780s, grain millers began making more use of windmills. In 1844, there were eight along the ridge to the east of the town, but almost all had disappeared by the early 1900s, thanks to the introduction of steam power (which also gave Mansfield this lovely smoggy haze).

22 Picture 21 showed Abraham's Mill at right and the Club or Rock Mill at left. This mill was built in 1778, on the site of an earlier post mill, as a co-operative venture by the town's 10 'Sick Clubs' or Friendly Societies, to help reduce flour prices. It is seen here from the east in 1872, behind the *Reindeer Inn*.

23 There were two basic types of windmill, the tower mills (locally called smock mills), as seen in the last picture, on which only the cap rotated to face the wind, and the cheaper post mills, which revolved as a unit on a central post. This post mill at the top of Skerry Hill may have been made as early as 1589.

24 In the 18th and 19th centuries, Mansfield was almost as important a centre of the malt industry as Newark. There were dozens of small maltings around the town, plus this surprisingly isolated building at West Hill on the Chesterfield Road (which caused endless financial headaches for its owner George Weightman in the early 19th century).

25 The famous Mansfield Brewery was founded in 1855, but for those who wanted softer drinks, very popular with the rise of the Temperance movement and the Salvation Army, there were numerous locally-made concoctions. The Metthams, proprietors of the *Eclipse Inn* in the marketplace until the early 1880s, made their fizzy drinks on Queen Street until about 1902, when they moved to Dame Flogan Street.

26 For those with more exotic tastes, there were 'botanical beers' or 'herb beers'. These could be obtained ready-made (in attractive stoneware jars if large quantities were required) from firms such as Stone's Westfield Botanical Brewery, or you could buy a handy packet mix. James Pegg, chemist of Church Street, was also advertising his 'Velvo' hand cream in 1899.

27 Midworth's foundry was one of several established during the Industrial Revolution. By 1824, they had a large site on Leeming Street, which remained in use until 1903, by then trading as Sanderson & Robinson. Mr Buxton photographed the premises shortly before the move to a new complex off Sutton Road, which evidently came none too soon.

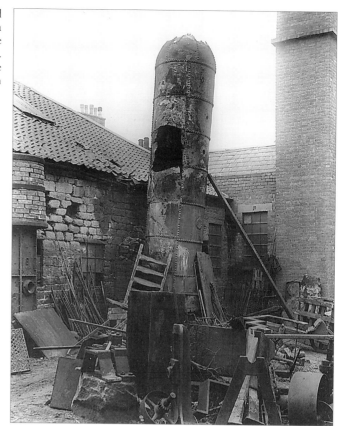

28 In 1852-3, a former tannery by the Water Meadows on the River Maun was converted to an iron foundry. Though the initial partnership of Bradshaw and Sansom failed in 1869, the new Meadow Foundry Company took the business successfully through the next century. Mr Buxton's Edwardian view is taken from the adjoining park paddling pool.

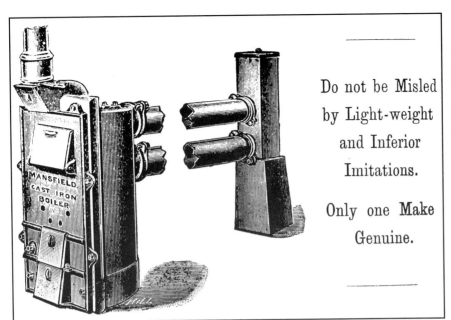

Do not be Misled
by Light-weight
and Inferior
Imitations.

Only one **Make**
Genuine.

29 Here is a typical product from the golden age of iron-founding in Mansfield. By the 1880s there were some 10 foundries in the town making use of the superb moulding sand quarried near Berry Hill. The compact 'Mansfield' boiler, made by Sansom's Union Foundry off Union Street, was popular for use in greenhouses.

30 Given its location in Sherwood Forest, Mansfield has of course always had some sort of timber trade. Like the foundries, however, the timber-yards only became truly industrialised in the late 18th century, after the invention of the circular saw in Southampton. Pye's moved to this Victoria Street site from Rock Valley about 1875.

31   The site of Pye's old sawmill (which had burned down in 1873) was added to the packing department of Barringer & Brown's mustard factory, descended from another earlier Rock Valley firm founded by Dickinson Ellis early in the 19th century. In 1889 they opened a new tin box factory on a site nearby.

32   The illustrious forerunner of Barringer's decorated tins? Between 1799 and 1802 William Billingsley, one of the greatest ceramic painters in history, lived and worked in a small house on Belvedere Street (demolished to build the Picturedrome in 1919). Though best known for his delicate flowers, he also painted miniature views such as these, now in Mansfield Museum.

33 During the Royal Visit in June 1914, Queen Mary was somewhat perturbed to see young girls working with heavy machinery at Barringer's. This photo appeared in several newspapers at the time. It must be pointed out, though, that the firm were traditional Quaker employers, providing a range of benefits for their workers.

34 This book contains no pictures of collieries, because there were none in the Borough of Mansfield (they were built just over the Mansfield Woodhouse border, to keep the rates bill down). This diagram shows why the Sherwood and 'Mansfield' pits were not sunk until the beginning of the 20th century: the sloping strata made it easier to mine further west.

35 Finally, if you want to know which are the leading lights of commerce in your community, try holding a charity fête. The programmes for these fairs and galas are filled with adverts for firms which are keen to emphasise their local presence: the three here (plus picture 74) are all taken from this 1937 booklet.

36 First, a firm which was then in its infancy, already making an impact. Founded by Alfred H. Whiteley in 1926, the firm moved in 1932 to the former Portland cotton mill on Victoria Street, which it still occupies in 2005. In 1937 they were also making the cabinets for their radios in what had been the Y.M.C.A., by the gasworks on Church Lane.

Devonshire Footwear

PRODUCED IN MANSFIELD
BY LOCAL CRAFTSMEN

Black Suede Calf 2 eye tie
Plateau Model Also
obtainable in Brown and
Coronation Blue

Black Suede Calf Court. Bow
Trimming. Also obtainable
in Brown, Coronation Blue
and Green

BUY DEVONSHIRE SHOES & SUPPORT LOCAL INDUSTRY

Sole Manufacturers—MANSFIELD SHOE Co. Ltd.

37 Here are some of the Mansfield Shoe Company's products of the time. The 'Devonshire' brand name was introduced in 1908, and in the mid-1930s the company became a founder-member of the Norvic group (from which it was rescued following a financial disaster in 1981, only to fail in 2004).

38 One problem for Mansfield Brewery has always been that another local firm stole the figure of Robin Hood for their corporate logo; this demanded a fair amount of ingenuity in advertising over the years, but the results were quite worthwhile. The Brewery remained independent almost to the end of the 20th century, though it was closed by new owners in 2001.

MANSFIELD ALES

"WORTH HUNTING FOR"

Mansfield Brewery Co., Ltd.

Trade and Commerce

39 Until 1840 the Moot Hall, seen here on the right, dominated Mansfield's small triangular marketplace. The subsequent clearances, exposing the new Town Hall of 1836, and the building of this memorial to Lord George Bentinck of Welbeck, reduced the status of the old hall, as this 1861 view (perhaps the oldest surviving Mansfield photograph) shows.

40 Because Mansfield was a royal manor before the 17th century, markets were held under Crown prerogative. When the manor was offered for sale in 1602, local traders were worried that the new owner would damage the market by imposing high tolls. In the long term, however, it survived.

41 These two photographs by Mr Buxton, probably taken about 1913, show the market much as we see it today, albeit with rather tatty stall canopies. Though an indoor market was provided when the Town Hall was built, the extended marketplace with its ranks of stalls is one of the glories of the town.

42 Livestock sales were kept separately from the main market, formerly on West Gate around the sundial now mistakenly called the 'Market Cross'. In 1877, though, a new Cattle Market was opened on the Water Meadows, by Nottingham Road, which remained in business for over a century. This A.S. Buxton photograph was taken c.1900.

43 Like many others throughout the country, Mansfield's tradesmen sometimes resorted to having their own 'token coins' made, when real money was scarce. Here are both sides of three half-penny tokens, actually about the size of a modern penny, issued in the 1660s by mercer Gregory Sylvester, felter Robert Wood (whose symbol is a felt cap) and carrier William Hurst.

44   In the 1870s William Sargent wrote the following description of town crier George Brown, proclaimer of official and commercial messages:

'Whenever he rings, jolly news it brings
And we all admire the crier;
Good Master Brown, of great renown,
He works for seller and buyer.'

45 Some Mansfield merchants had wider ambitions than mere shopkeeping. Charles Thompson made a fortune on commercial trips across Europe and the Near East. He rescued his single-cup teapot from the ruins of the Portuguese capital Lisbon, where he barely survived the great earthquake of 1755. The damage you see here is due to 20th-century clumsiness!

46 Having retired to his home town to dispense much of his wealth on charitable work, Thompson died in 1784 and was buried, during a snowstorm, in a site of his own choosing: his favourite viewpoint on high ground by the Southwell road. The grave remains, but 20th-century housing has obscured the panorama.

47 'Blake and Beeley' were still selling hardware beside and beneath the viaduct on Church Street until 1996, over a century after this engraving was published in 1889. Much else has changed: the new Town Mill is gone from the background, and most of the small buildings lower down the street have been replaced.

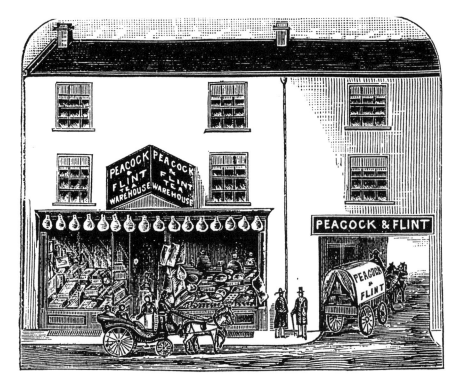

48 From the same 1889 guide to Nottinghamshire commerce, here are the premises of the short-lived partnership of Peacock & Flint, established about 1885 on West Gate. By 1893 they had split, with Flint continuing to trade from West Gate while Peacock had a shop behind the Moot Hall, in Angel Yard.

49 Much of West Gate remained residential until early in the 20th century. This photo shows how the gothic-influenced house 'Moss Hall', by the old cattle-market sundial, was converted for retail purposes. The small building at left, designed by Fothergill Watson in 1875, was the front of a large auction-room; the even smaller dry-cleaners was added some years later.

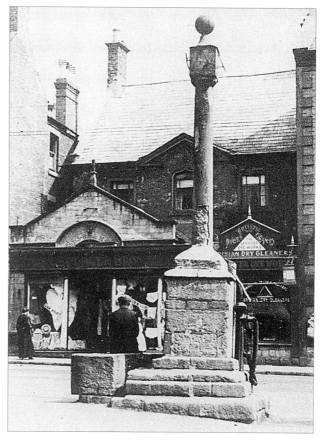

50 The back gardens and yards of premises on the north side of West Gate led up to Back Lane, beyond which, originally, were fields. This lane was gradually developed during the 19th century, ultimately being renamed 'Clumber Street'. It had become a classic low-rent shopping area, as this view of its north side shows.

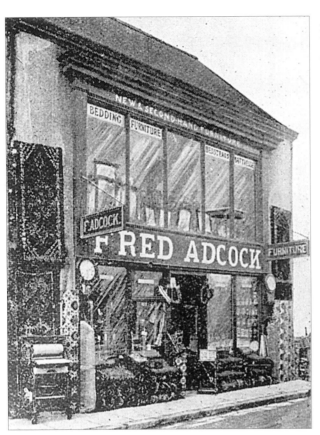

51 Development on Back Lane's south side had been a matter of filling up former West Gate back gardens with buildings – very profitable for the landowners. Here is part of a 1903 advert for one of the shops thus created, near the corner of Clumber Street and Leeming Street. Upfront displays and low prices were the keys to Adcock's success.

52 While low-rent areas like Clumber Street attracted specialists and discounters, the main roads radiating from the marketplace provided for both essential shopping and premium goods. George Munks, for example, had a tailor's shop on Westgate. In the mid-1890s his wife, Marie, found herself in charge, and ran the shop successfully for many years.

53 A similar story can be told of this shop. Henry Morris the butcher had occupied the ancient building seen at the beginning of the 'Town House' chapter (picture 75). It seems to have been his wife who made the move about 1903 to this smaller, but smart and hygienic-looking, shop on Wood Street, then a fast-developing residential area.

54 (*below left*)   Here is a butcher's shop left over from an earlier age, typical of the open stalls which once lined the ancient unextended marketplace. This shack in Stockwell Gate, painted here by Mr Buxton, was adapted for the trade after the old stalls were demolished – it had previously been a barber's!

55 (*below right*)   Buxton may have painted the butcher's stall from memory; it stood at the far right of this chaotic scene, which he photographed during demolition for the extension of the Co-op store. The Co-op had stood on Queen Street since 1866, but expanded to Stockwell Gate in 1907-8.

56 Back on Stockwell Gate, *c.*1910, on the left is the site of the multi-storey car park, a parade of shops built in 1906. On the right are some much older buildings: the former malthouse which was decorated in the 1920s with fake half-timbering to become Ye Olde Crowne (later Stockwells) and, just to its left, a real Tudor house.

57 A successful chemist's business in the marketplace area was William Jackson's, number 1 Stockwell Gate. This was taken over about 1890 by Philip Shacklock, whose family ran it for many years. This view of the crowded interior is from an advert published in 1931.

58 In a book such as this, we must not forget the photographers. There were two commercial photographers in Mansfield by the late 1850s, but they probably concentrated on portraits. The Sherwood Photographic Company, whose Westgate studio is shown here about 1909, were responsible for many of the best Edwardian photographs of the town.

59 Before the railway age, travellers would have stayed at town-centre inns such as the *Swan* or the *Nag's Head*. After the creation of the Worksop and Southwell lines, however, accommodation was provided near to the station. The *Midland Hotel* was converted in the 1870s from a gentleman's residence, the new station having been built in its former garden.

MANSFIELD SAVINGS' BANK.

Is open every Monday from eleven o'clock until one o'clock.

Interest at the rate of £3 0s. 10d. per cent., allowed upon all sums when they amount to fifteen shillings.

The interest due to each Depositor is calculated to the first of November, and either paid on application or is placed as principal to the account.

Deposits may be made of not less than one shilling and not exceeding thirty pounds in the whole in one year, ending the 20th of November.

No greater sum than £150 can be taken from any Depositor, which may remain at interest until it amounts to £200.

Friendly Societies may deposit within the year to any amount.

A Depositor (before making his or her first Deposit) must sign a Declaration according to a form given in Rule 10, that he or she has not any money in any other Savings' Bank. A Depositor having money in more than one Savings' Bank at the same time, is liable to forfeit and lose all right and title to the same.

Application for money must be made at the Bank, either by the Depositor in person or by a written order according to the form given, which order must be signed by the Depositor in the presence of a Witness. See Rule 27.

This Duplicate is to be produced when any money is deposited in or drawn out of the Bank, and it must be presented at the Bank after 20th November in every year for the purpose of being examined and perfected.

60 Commerce cannot function easily without credit. Though private loans were common, the Mansfield Bank was founded in 1802 as an offshoot of the Nottingham partnership Moore, Maltby, Evans & Middlemore. In common with other banks at the time, it issued its own banknotes. This version from about 1816 depicts the Greendale Oak at Welbeck.

61 The early commercial banks were run for businessmen by the gentry, but a Savings Bank movement soon developed. The Mansfield Savings Bank was established in 1818. Its enlarged offices by the Town Hall, opened in 1843, became redundant 20 years later, when it merged with the national Post Office Savings Bank, and were converted into a County Court.

Transport

62   Though Mansfield became the hub of a complex network of turnpike roads during the Industrial Revolution, these were still not adequate to move heavy goods. The hilly terrain made a canal impractical, so in 1817-19 a railway was built to the existing canal wharf at Pinxton. The catch was that the line as built was not suitable for locomotives.

63   In the late 1840s, mercifully, the Pinxton line was taken over by the Midland Railway, who extended the track to Nottingham, and provided steam power. In the late 1860s, several improvements were made, notably the smoothing of curves by building this timber viaduct at the Hermitage, to replace the Portland Bridge at King's Mill.

64 Timber and water are not an ideal combination, and the Hermitage viaduct was probably intended only to be temporary. Here, about 1900, a diver is seen leaning on his air-pump at the beginning of the operation to replace the 1860s viaduct with the stone bridge still used in 2005 on the revived 'Robin Hood Line'.

65   When the Midland Railway made additional connections to Worksop and Southwell in 1869-75, temporary structures were not appropriate. The engineering quality was superb, using local stone, often in an intriguing irregular pattern, to create features like this bridge over the River Maun at Quarry Lane, photographed as new in about 1871.

66   To match the line of the new viaduct across the town, the company had also to build a new station, replacing the old building on Station Street and accessed by a new road round the elegant Broom House (the hotel shown in picture 59). Here is the Belvedere Street entrance to the station from the opening souvenir album, about 1872.

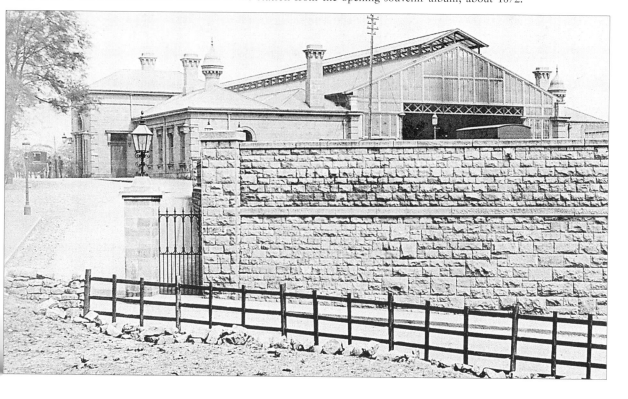

67 In the 1881 census, William Warren, aged 72, is still described as a 'Railway Pointsman'. Here he is, perhaps a few years earlier, with his safety flag, taking time off from his business of ensuring that trains moved around the station and its sidings without incident.

68 Within the town, transport remained a matter of animal – or human – power. Mansfield's light-engineering firms, used to making complex machinery for the textile industry, found the transition to cycle manufacture easy, and might have prospered today if the same process had not also happened in Nottingham.

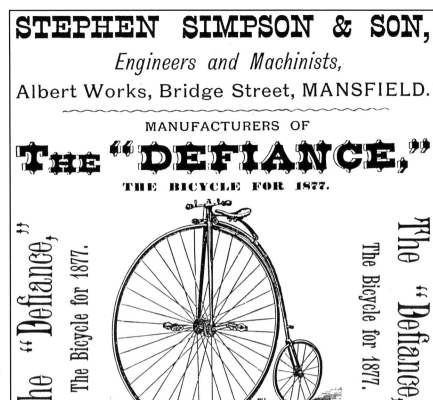

STEPHEN SIMPSON & SON,

Engineers and Machinists,

Albert Works, Bridge Street, MANSFIELD.

MANUFACTURERS OF

THE "DEFIANCE,"

THE BICYCLE FOR 1877.

The "Defiance," The Bicycle for 1877.

The "Defiance," The Bicycle for 1877.

69 In 1898, an experiment with a steam-powered bus proved disastrous, and local businessmen began agitating for the creation of a tramway system. When the town's power-station was built in 1903, it was designed to be capable of supplying such a system, and by 1905 the main streets were being dug up to lay rails.

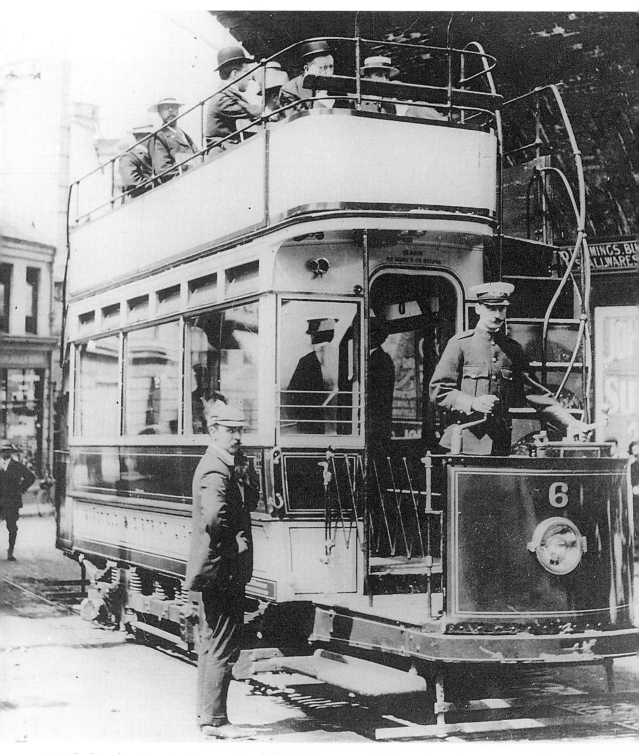

70　The line along Leeming Street to Mansfield Woodhouse, seen in the previous picture, was actually made in 1906, but here is an early view of the first line to be opened in July 1905. This tram is passing under the viaduct on the way to Albert Street and Nottingham Road. The other original lines led to Sutton and Pleasley Hill.

71 The trams were stopped almost as soon as they had started by a strike in 1906. The company management handled the situation with considerable lack of competence, leading to some ugly scenes, and only the intervention of the mayor of Mansfield brought some sense to the situation.

72 One advantage of the trams was that, provided the power-supply was not overloaded, they worked happily in almost any conditions (though they did occasionally run away on the steeper sections of the network, such as Skerry Hill). Here a flood stretching from Norfolk Drive down Westgate to the Maun, probably in May 1932, presents no problems.

73 The internal combustion engine revived the idea of large-capacity bus transport early in the 20th century, and many places around Mansfield that were not served by train or tram soon benefited from the new services, many of which departed from the top of Westgate, by the Congregational Church.

74 In 1932, the inflexible tram network was closed and double-decker buses were brought in to serve the town routes, still using the old tram depot on Sutton Road. This 1937 advert indicates how the company grew rapidly to meet the various travel demands of an age when private cars were still a luxury.

The Town House ...

75   This long, low range of buildings on Westgate, seen here about 1900 (and demolished just before 1930 to make way for the Plaza Cinema), was almost the last of what must have been a common type of farmstead in Mansfield 400 years before, shared by humans and beasts.

76 In Tudor and Stuart Mansfield, some of the town's best houses were built on the steeply-rising ground at the bottom of Ratcliffe Gate. This, in Lime Tree Place, was home in the 18th century to the Burden family of textile entrepreneurs. It is seen here in 1902, shortly before demolition.

77 'Lime Tree Place' is not, as some suppose, the name of the last-mentioned house, but of the short road in which it stood. Here is another once-elegant old residence further along, which in the 19th century became home to the manager of the gas-works (glimpsed at right), but by 1902 was used for storage.

78 The industrialisation of Lime Tree Place was, perhaps, poetic justice. Here, next to the site of the Burdens' bleach works on Church Lane (used as a timber-yard when this photo was taken, about 1906), are the homes of some of their workers.

79 These two cottages (pictured by Mr Buxton) stood in 'Dragon Court', a steep alley which led up from Church Street behind the houses of Leeming Street. This court seems to have been a 17th-century example of the tendency, more common a hundred years later, to convert back gardens into building plots.

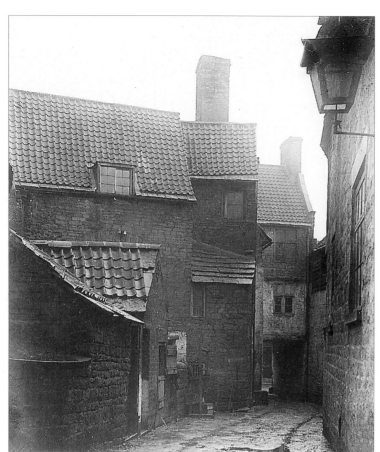

80 Here is another garden which became a building site, the back of what had been the home of late 17th-century businessman Samuel Brunts on Church Street, more familiar when this photo was taken, about 1910, as the *Old Eight Bells* pub. The yard makes an odd angle because it follows the original course of the Lady Brook down towards the Maun.

81 Something of the same cramming tendency can be seen here, at the point where Church Street becomes Bridge Street, with the two houses at right on an almost triangular plot in front of what was originally a building set obliquely to the street. The artist may be J. Seddon Tyrer.

82 Where Toothill, overlooking Church Street, did not actually form a cliff, some ingenious householders managed to create gardens on the hillside. This little summer-house, directly above the houses in the last picture, was a feature of the once-splendid garden behind a house on Toothill Lane.

83 Here is an equally ambitious front garden, in an equally surprising location. Mr Buxton's art has hidden a great deal here, for this house was just off Queen Street, backing onto the yard of the *Swan Inn*. The garden had been twice this size, but it was to shrink still further as the demand for shops grew in late Victorian times.

84 Many front gardens, however, survived well into the 20th century. Here is the sundial house on Bridge Street, just after the First World War. The sundial seen in recent years is higher up the wall – indeed the whole frontage has needed heavy restoration due to an insensitive shop conversion.

85   Apart from ribbon development, the first real growth of the
town was at the beginning of the
19th century, when new roads such
as Union Street and Catlow Street
(later St John Street) were created
on a green-field site. The Birch
family are seen here, *c*.1905, in their
spacious garden at Oakdene on St
John Street.

86   Keep a look-out for Mansfield's
most familiar architectural features.
On the left in this scene near the
top of Leeming Street, the windows
have stone 'mullion' pillars, while the
building on the right has the sash
windows with heavy stone surrounds
which began to replace mullions in
the late 18th century.

87 The houses in the last photograph were occupied by wealthy tradesmen (including 18th-century merchant Charles Thompson) but here, next to a former tannery on the Maun, is Meadow Row, a grim huddle of workers' cottages, pictured shortly after the Great Central Railway embankment had been built across their backyards in 1911-13.

88 If the Industrial Revolution was a time of cramming in, thanks to the need to preserve farmland, the 20th century was a time of outward movement. Here, at the corner of Bath Lane and Leeming Street in 1902, several small houses are about to be demolished to make way for the Grand Theatre, later a cinema.

... and the Country House

89 Even in the 'mining boom' years of the early 20th century the built-up area of Mansfield was only about five square kilometres (compared with about eighteen in 2005), as this view along Southwell Road, near the junction with Jenny Beckett's Lane, dramatically demonstrates. Urban spread is not, however, an entirely modern phenomenon.

90 Though very few houses were built outside the urban heart of Mansfield until the 18th century, once the great open fields had been enclosed the owners of the new 'closes' often equipped them with barns and other buildings. 'The White House' on Ladybrook Lane (here painted by W. Daws, about 1920) probably began in this way.

91 To give you an idea of how small an area the town occupied until the 20th century, here is St John's Church, as seen from near the junction of Ladybrook Lane and Westfield Lane by J. Seddon Tyrer, about 1867. Just to its right, on the hill-top, is the windmill which used to stand on Lurchill, above Leeming Street.

92   Though the town was so compact, there was some 'ribbon development', particularly along Chesterfield Road, in the late 18th and early 19th centuries. Most of the best houses stood on the hillside east of the road, but some respectable smaller houses were built at the road's edge, such as this one, which occupied the site of the later Catholic Church.

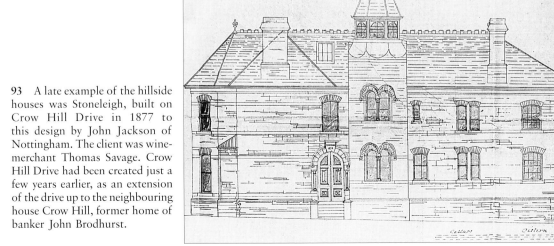

93   A late example of the hillside houses was Stoneleigh, built on Crow Hill Drive in 1877 to this design by John Jackson of Nottingham. The client was wine-merchant Thomas Savage. Crow Hill Drive had been created just a few years earlier, as an extension of the drive up to the neighbouring house Crow Hill, former home of banker John Brodhurst.

94   Another odd exception to the practice of building to the east of Chesterfield Road was Beech Hill, built about 1870 and home in its early years to the wealthy sisters Jane and Sarah Eadson. The long garden down to Chesterfield Road was designed with a shrubbery (seen on the left) between the house and the main lawn.

95   Except for the cottages of the quarry workers near the present *Pheasant Inn* there were few humble homes along Chesterfield Road. Here, near the site of the modern lesiure centre, are some exceptions. The odd roof galleries suggest that they were built for weavers, perhaps as early as the 17th century.

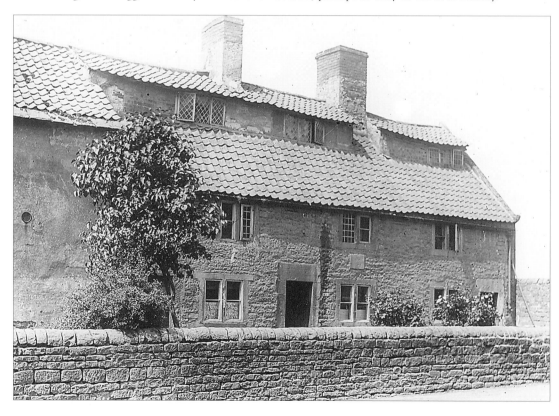

96 The managers, and in some cases the owners, of Mansfield's textile mills tended to live fairly close to the works. The house of the proprietors of Hermitage Mill, seen here in a faded photo of about 1900, may actually be on the site of the original Hermitage, a country retreat built for 13th-century bishop Thomas Bek.

97 Here is an Edwardian view of another house with a pleasant view over the millpond, by Stanton's Mill on Bath Lane. 'Bath Vale' was probably always a manager's house, as the Stanton family possessed ample and elegant accommodation elsewhere.

98 The Stantons had been partners with the Burdens at the Church Lane bleachyard, so they lived in a house by the Water Meadows. In 1803, however, they had this modest mansion built at Carr Bank, overlooking their Bath Lane mill. It is pictured here shortly before its conversion to offices and Art School in 1921.

99 Before travelling further out to the countryside, we must see the famous Rock Houses at the top of Ratcliffe Gate. This 1848 sketch shows them at their fullest development, with many of the caves hidden behind substantial house frontages. At that time there were some two dozen Rock Houses here, in two rows on the hillside.

100 Most of the Rock Houses were abandoned between 1880 and 1890, probably due to the more stringent health standards of late Victorian times. Perhaps surprisingly this substantial structure, fronting the road, was not the last to be occupied; widower John Bramwell lived in a little cave higher up the hills until his death in 1900.

101 The grandest of Mansfield's country houses is also one of the earliest. There may have been a house at Berry Hill by the end of the 17th century, and for much of the 18th it was home to William Bilbie, who was Sheriff of Nottinghamshire in 1778-9 and died in 1784. This engraving by Malcolm & Eastgate was published about 1800.

102 After a period of uncertainty following Bilbie's death, Berry Hill was home to the Walker family for much of the 19th century, then (from 1889 to 1920) the Hollins family, owners of the Pleasley Vale textile mills. Its history after that date belongs to another chapter (see picture 147).

103 Was this curious structure (painted by Seddon Tyrer) built in the 17th century by a man seeking to avoid the plagues which periodically ravaged Britain's towns? So one historian was told in the 1890s, but I suspect that such an elegant building, on a hilltop within strolling distance of Berry Hill Hall, was really a summer-house.

Education

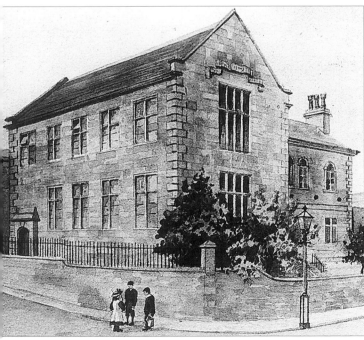

104 In 1552, a cottage by St Peter's churchyard was given to the churchwardens for the purpose of creating a town school. In 1561, Queen Elizabeth I authorised the formation of a Grammar School bearing her name, and for 300 years it stood on the same site. Though the school has moved, the buildings as rebuilt in 1715 still stand.

105 Education in Mansfield was encouraged by several later charitable benefactors. In 1725, Faith Clerkson left money in her will to fund this school for boys and girls, which stood at the corner of what we now call Albert Street and Station Street. Mr Buxton painted this charming view from one of his seediest photographs.

106 A few years before Faith Clerkson, Samuel Brunts had left money for educational purposes, and when joined in 1785 to a bequest from merchant Charles Thompson it was enough to build this school on Toothill Lane, ancestor of the present Brunts' School. The building still stands, but it is hidden by others.

107 Most schools in the 18th century were run on a commercial basis. One of Mansfield's grandest was Mrs Clarke's boarding school for girls, in the former mansion of Arthur Stanhope at the bottom of Ratcliffe Gate. Isabel Clarke moved here from Bramcote in 1770, and managed the school until her death in 1809.

108 When Mrs Clarke's heir sold Stanhope House (see picture 9), her successor Miss Creswell, with new partner Miss Hatton, moved to this smaller house opposite the old Grammar School and churchyard. Despite having a tannery, a foundry and a malthouse for neighbours, it was used by later teachers, such as artist Ann Paulson, for many years.

109 Equally unpromising in this Buxton photograph is Parsons' Yard off Westgate. What was once a beautiful house and garden had been encumbered in the late 18th century with a cotton mill, and other incongruous buildings were added later. Early in the 19th century the house and mill were owned by the Rev. John Parsons.

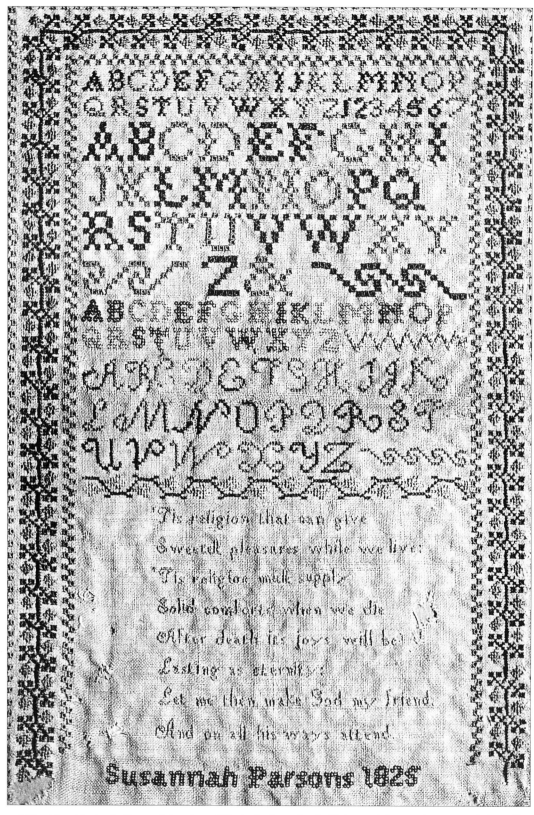

110 After his death, Parsons' daughters Elizabeth, Jane, Sarah, Helen and Susannah converted the mill to an elementary school, which they ran from about 1827 to 1877. Although the education was basic, it was very efficient, and many of the town's most prominent citizens sent their children there.

111 Queen Elizabeth's Grammar School, having declined over many years, was re-founded in 1877, with a new site off Chesterfield Road. An 'Elizabethan' style was chosen for the spacious new buildings, which were completed in 1879 at a cost of £10,000 (though the school had begun taking pupils in 1878). This 1932 drawing is by the headmaster, Leslie Burgess.

112 The re-foundation of the Grammar School also made possible the establishment of a Girls' Grammar School, for which a site on Woodhouse Road was provided by the Brunts' Charity. Provision of the buildings took some time, the first pupils being admitted in September 1891. The main hall was barrel-vaulted, and the theme was echoed elsewhere, as in this art room.

113   Because the development of Nottingham and Mansfield vastly increased the charity's income, Brunts' School itself was re-founded in 1894 as a Technical School, with much-expanded buildings almost opposite the Girls' Grammar School, for which Brunts' and Thompson's charities provided £5,000, plus an annual income of at least £500. This large science block was added in 1930.

114   Here is a science classroom of this period at the school: in this case, a biology room. The improvements were in the nick of time, as the needs of technical education had changed greatly since the 1890s. Indeed, 60 years later the whole site was abandoned, because the buildings themselves were becoming unstable.

THE RESULT OF AN UNEXPECTED MATHS. TEST UPON IVc.

115 Mansfield's secondary schools have a long tradition of producing school magazines, each with a unique flavour. *The Elizabethan*, produced at the Boys' Grammar School, included some wonderful artwork by both pupils and staff (see picture **111**). The Brunts' School magazine, however, took itself less seriously, and cartooning was encouraged.

116 Though Mansfield relied on charities and religious institutions to provide education before 1900, the Borough Council found itself forced to build schools as the population grew. High Oakham School, on Nottingham Road, was founded in 1926 as a secondary school – and the many photographs in its school magazine *Oak Leaves* show the practical emphasis of its curriculum in the 1930s.

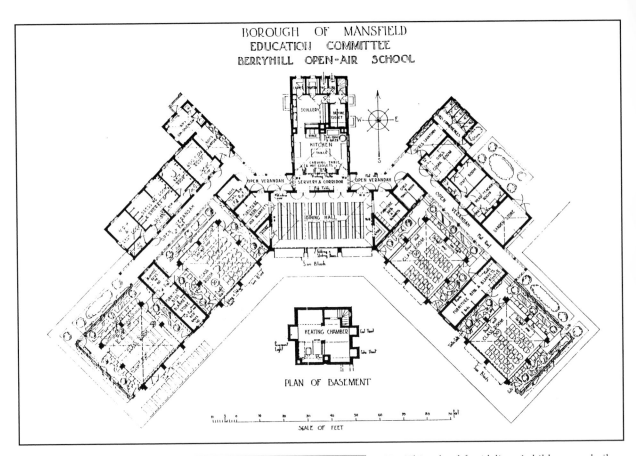

BOROUGH OF MANSFIELD
EDUCATION COMMITTEE
BERRYHILL OPEN-AIR SCHOOL

PLAN OF BASEMENT

SCALE OF FEET

117 This school for 'delicate' children was built in 1931. Its name was a result of the unusual plan of having folding and sliding doors which could effectively remove an entire wall of each classroom, allowing plenty of fresh air when the weather outside was not too cold. Beds were also provided for rest periods.

118 The dominant influence in A.S. Buxton's education was artist J. Seddon Tyrer, who gave art classes at the Mechanics' Institute. From these developed the School of Art, of which Buxton became headmaster in the 1890s. He guided the school for nearly 40 years, but died shortly after it finally found a permanent home on Chesterfield Road in 1930.

Entertainment and Leisure

Theatre, Mansfield.

On MONDAY Evening, June 16, 1800, will be prefented, a celebrated Hiftorical Tragedy, called, The

ROMAN FATHER;

OR THE
DELIVERER of his COUNTRY.

The great end of the Stage fhould be to improve and to inform. And the Bufinefs of the Tragic-Writer fhould be, to felect from the page of Hiftory, fuch brilliant paffages as may dignify and recommend the Principles of Virtue, Patriotifm and general Benevolence. To accomplifh thefe great purpofes there could not perhaps, thro' the extenfive round of Hiftoric exibition, be chofen a happier period and circumftances, than what gave rife to the prefent Tragedy.

The moment chofen by the judicious Author, is when the fate of ALBA and ROME is to be decided by the illuftrious Patriotifm of the HORATII and the CURIATII; each band being three Brothers, devoted by the facred Love of their refpective Countries, determine their deftiny by their own. This dignified fubject is made ftill more interefting by the fecret Love of the Sifter, of the Roman band towards one of the Alban band. In the diftreffing Struggles between HORATIA, her Patriotic FATHER, and her Victorious BROTHER, fuch affecting Sentiments and Situations arife, as muft place this effort among the beft of thofe Tragedies that give tendernefs to Virtue, and dignity to Feeling—Where the Mind can juftify by Principle, what the Heart has received with Senfibility.

Horatius, *(the Roman Father)*   Mr. CLARKE.
Tullus Hoftilius, *(King of Rome)*   Mr. CROSS.
Valerius, *(a young Patrician)*   Mr. YOUNG.
Roman Soldier,   Mr. PEIRCE.
Cautus,   Mr. HUGGINS.   Vindicus,   Mr. COLLIER.
Publius Horatius, *(the deliverer of his Country)*   Mr. HENRY.
Horatia, *(her firft Appearance)*   Mifs COLLIER.
Valeria,   Mrs. STANNARD.

TRIUMPHAL ENTRY of *PUBLIUS HORATIUS* into ROME,

Preceded by VIRGINS ftrewing FLOWERS, attended by the NOBLES, GENERALS, and GUARDS, bearing the TROPHIES, BANNERS, STANDARDS, &c. as in LONDON, the Mufic playing, with a full CHORUS,
" See the Conquering Hero comes."

Preceding the PLAY, a PROLOGUE, written for the Occafion, by Mr. COLLIER.

A COMIC SONG, by Mr. CROSS.

To which will be added, a reviv'd FARCE, called

Fortune's Frolic.

Robin Roughead,   Mr. HUGGINS.   Snacks,   Mr. PEIRCE.
Clown,   Mr. CROSS.   Villager,   Mr. STANNARD.
Rattle,   Mr. HENRY.   Frank,   Mr. YOUNG.
Mifs Nancy,   Mrs. STANNARD.   Dolly,   Mrs. CLARK.   Margery,   Mrs. PEIRCE.

BENJAMIN ROBINSON, PRINTER, &c. MARKET-PLACE, MANSFIELD.

119   The Theatre, in a yard next to the *Swan Inn*, was built about 1780 by William McLellan, a joiner and builder who needed a hall for his sideline as an auctioneer. The first recorded performance, Sheridan's 'School for Scandal', was by special request from the officers of the Nottinghamshire Militia in 1783.

JENNINGS'

Alexandra Theatre, WHITE HART CROFT, Mansfield.

ESTABLISHED 60 YEARS.

Sole Proprietor and Manager . . . . . Mr. GEORGE JENNINGS.

On TUESDAY, FEBRUARY 11th,

For the BENEFIT of Mr. & Mrs. HARRY WYNNE

Under the *PATRONAGE* of the

SHERWOOD LODGE, No. 1687, Mansfield I.O. of ODD-FELLOWS, M.U.

When will be produced the Splendid Military Drama, with Magnificent Dresses, entitled—

DEATH OR GLORY

Or, THE CHILD OF THE BATTLEFIELD.

CORPORAL FRANCOIS, the Dumb Soldier   Mr. H. WYNNE

Concluding with the MUSICAL COMEDY in one Act, entitled—

THE WATERMAN.

TOM TUG, with Songs, "The Jolly Young Waterman," "Farewell my Trim Built Wherry," and "The Bay of Biscay," Miss VIOLA JENNINGS
ROBIN, with Song "Cherry and Plums"   Mr. C. FORTESCUE

120   The Theatre was far too small for 19th-century spectaculars. Some performances were held in the new Town Hall, but the most popular venues were the mobile theatres which set up in White Hart Croft each winter. This sample from a very long 1896 poster shows that the entertainment on offer had changed little since 1800.

121   The Fair, held each summer on the feast of Mansfield's patron saints Peter and Paul, was begun by Royal Charter in 1377 as an occasion for specialist traders to gather in the town. The gradual development of permanent shops reduced the necessity for such occasions, so the sideshows ultimately became the fair's sole purpose.

122 Celebrations for the 550th anniversary of the Fair, and 700th of the market charter, in July 1927 were captured on what may be the earliest surviving Mansfield movie. These scenes show the presentation of a nine-kilo gooseberry 'pork pie' (an old fair-time delicacy) at the Town Hall, and the children's medieval pageant held at the Field Mill stadium.

123 Inns and alehouses have been part of Mansfield life far longer than the Fair. Even the *New Inn*, seen at right in this Buxton painting of an 1880s scene, actually dates from about 1831 and probably opened as a result of a government attempt to encourage people to drink beer rather than spirits.

124 On the east side of Church Street, many premises were dug straight back into the hillside, the caves providing naturally cool storage for commodities such as alcoholic drinks. The old *White Lion* pub, seen here about 1902, just before its closure, had cellars dug deep into the rock, leading back from this underground laundry.

125 The Leeming Street *Bowl in Hand*, seen at left, was probably built in the late 17th century, during the revival of popular entertainment which followed the Restoration of the Monarchy. Behind the two cottages which dominate this picture is the reason for the pub's existence, a bowling-green still in use today.

126 The bars on one window have led to the suggestion that this building at one end of the bowling-green, pictured about 1900, was used as a magistrates' court, but it was always described as a summer-house. The magistrates are more likely to have met in the large assembly hall, of which one supporting pillar can be seen at left.

127 Though the public bowling-green was attached to the *Bowl in Hand*, other pubs naturally fielded teams. Just across the road, for example, is the *Horse and Jockey*, and here we see their proud team celebrating Empire Day in 1911.

128 A golf course was established in 1895 on the high ground north of Ravensdale, overlooking the Maun valley (in effect, a very deep bunker). It was replaced by the larger Sherwood Golf Club in 1912-13, but as this 1907 sketch, one of an interesting series by A.A. Richardson, shows, the old course had its attractions.

129 Cricket has been played in Mansfield since the 18th century, and in late Victorian times a permanent pitch was provided next to the Field Mill. Here we see the local team at the ground, about 1900. You will perhaps have guessed that it became customary to use the ground for football in winter ...

Mansfield Town Football Club.

OFFICIAL PROGRAMME

Vol. 4. SEASON 1931-32. Saturday, Sept. 5th, 1931. **Two Pence.**

Patron—C. W. Chadburn, Esq. President—F. Oliver, Esq. Life Members—J. Birks, Esq. A. E. Champion, Esq.
Chairman—G. Annable, Esq. Vice-Chairman—H Smalley, Esq.
Directors—F. E Nash, Esq., W. H. Jackson, Esq , F. Allen, Esq., W. Priestley, Esq , J. H. Peet, Esq., W. W. Fenton, Esq.,
G. Baxter, Esq., A. C. Shillington, Esq., G. E. Hardy, Esq., G, Wragg, Esq.,
Assistant Secretary—S. Musgrave. Secretary-Manager—J G. Hickling.
Registered Office—Field Mill Ground Tel. No. 567. Colours—Blue Jerseys, White Knickers.

MR. GEORGE ANNABLE.
Chairman of Mansfield Town
Football Club, who to-day is
a proud man at seeing one of
his greatest ambitions reali-
sed—the Town competing in
English League Football.

GEORGE BLACKBURN
(Captain),
the former Aston Villa and
Cardiff City half-back, has
been appointed Captain of
Mansfield Town and should
prove a pillar of strength
to the Town.

130 The current occupants of the Field Mill Stadium, Mansfield Town Football Club, are descended
from 'Mansfield Wesleyans', a successful team in the early years of the 20th century. Though
the team seems to have begun playing as M.T.F.C. in 1910, 1931-2 was their first season in the
Football League (Division 3, to be precise).

131 Mansfield's first public leisure amenity, in the sense of being provided with no thought of profit, was the recreation ground on the Water Meadows, opened in 1880. Initially, the development was little more than a matter of tidying up the river channel and improving the ground, but more facilities were provided from the 1890s.

132 In the early years of the 20th century the recreation ground gained a bowling-green, with a little pavilion (still there at the beginning of the 21st) and children's swings given by the mayor in 1906. In 1914, the 21st birthday of the heir to the Duke of Portland was the occasion on which it was given the name Titchfield Park. This view dates from the 1920s.

133   W.E. Bailey, heir to most of the Mansfield Brewery's profits, opened his natural history collection to the public at his home on Westgate in the 1870s, but took it with him when poor health forced a move to Cornwall. He gave the collection to the town of Mansfield just before his death in 1903, and it formed the nucleus of Mansfield Museum.

134   By the 1930s the corrugated-iron building which Bailey had provided was beyond repair, so the Museum was closed from 1935 to 1938, when the main part of the present building was opened on 19 October with a lively and stimulating speech by the mayor, Councillor Mrs M.E. Marriott. The revived institution had nearly 50,000 visitors in the next five months.

Civic Amenities and Civic Pride

135 For most of its history, the driving force behind Mansfield's community pride has been the gentry, those wealthy citizens who owned the land and major businesses, and from 1823 were elected as 'Improvement Commissioners'. Here is industrialist John Ellis's triumphal arch on Leeming Street to celebrate the 1832 Reform Act, painted by Mrs Ann Paulson.

136 In a field off the Old Newark Road, south of the town, stands a reminder of much earlier administrators. The (probably upside-down) pillar seems to commemorate a meeting of Sherwood Forest officials in 1702, but may be much older. These visitors in October 1930 are the Old Mansfield Society, including A.S. Buxton with moustache and light raincoat.

137 The movement towards providing an Improvement Commission, achieved in 1823, arguably began in 1815, with the establishment of a town fire station on Toothill Lane. This picture from the 1920s shows what was then the town's most modern fire-engine alongside a hand-pumped machine of the type that would have been used in the early 19th century.

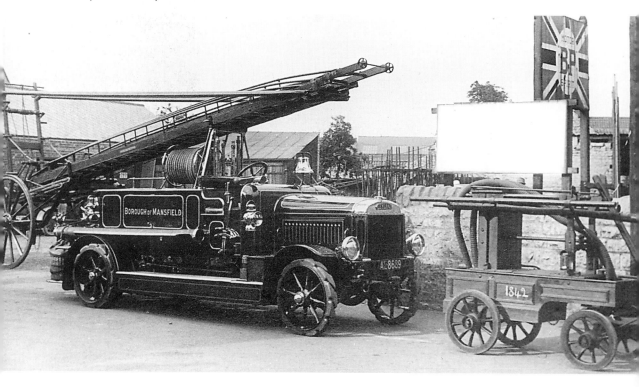

138 The fire station remained on Toothill Lane until 1939, when a much-expanded complex was opened on the extension of Rosemary Street, near the Chesterfield Road (this photo was the centrefold of the opening brochure). The 'new' building has been demolished in its turn, for replacement in 1996.

139 When the new Town Hall was opened in 1836, it included at the rear a covered market, and the building with the tiny semi-circular window seen to its right in this early view by art teacher Ann Paulson: a lock-up for local felons. In the yard between that and the Town Hall was a small house for a constable.

140 Another early public service in Mansfield was the gas supply, which began in 1824 from a site off Ratcliffe Gate. Initially provided by a private consortium, the service was later bought by the Improvement Commissioners, who had been major customers since 1825, when they provided the town's first gas street-lamps.

141 The previous picture, taken by Mr Buxton about 1919, shows one of the great telescopic gas-holders on the extension of the gas-works by Church Lane. Here is another of the improvements made after the business passed into public control, the 1901 set of 'tower scrubbers' (made by the Union Foundry), which removed impurities from the gas.

142　Another private-enterprise utility which the Improvement Commissioners felt obliged to take into their control was water supply. The first pumping-station, opened in 1872 off Nottingham Road, produced unpleasant 'hard' water, so the Commissioners bought the company and spent £70,000 building this new waterworks at Rainworth in 1897.

143　Youngest of the town's basic services is the electricity supply. This power station was built by the Borough Council off Lime Tree Place in 1902-3, intended to supply not only domestic and industrial customers, but the proposed tram network. Designed to very high standards, it incorporated a refuse incinerator. This view is from the south end of the works.

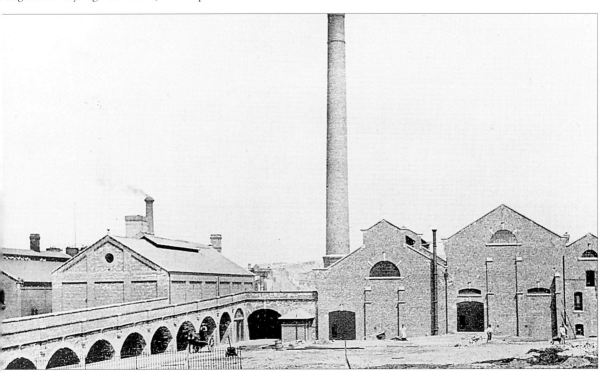

Mansfield Forest Encroachments.

Notice is hereby given,

THAT a Meeting of the Copyholders having right of Common on the **FOREST** within the Manor and Parish of **MANSFIELD**, will be held at the MOOT-HALL, in Mansfield on *Monday* the **24th day** of *May* instant, at **11** o'Clock in the Forenoon, to take into consideration and to determine on the most proper steps to be adopted, with the concurrence of the Lord of the said Manor, for abating and removing the Encroachments on the said Forest.

By Order of the Lord of the Manor and Committee of Copyholders,

GEO. WALKDEN,
Steward of the Manor,

RICHD. PARSONS,
WM. WOODCOCK,
Solicitors to the Committee.

Mansfield, May 17th, 1830.

COLLINSON, PRINTER.

144 Contrary to popular misconception, shares in most commons were limited to those who could claim ancient rights attached to the houses they owned. In Mansfield, the lucky few made strenuous attempts to protect their privileges against those who tried to make fields on the open Forest commons, until their own shares were officially fenced in 1853.

145 Surprisingly, Mansfield's first hospital was not opened until 1881 (though for 14 years the town had shared facilities at Mansfield Woodhouse). The town made up for lost time though, and became home to several regional institutions in addition to its General Hospital. Here is a recently-opened extension of the Ransom Sanatorium, about 1925.

146 The Sanatorium (opened in 1902 as the Sherwood Forest Sanatorium, but renamed a few years later after its late physician, Dr William B. Ransom of Nottingham) was a county-wide facility specialising in the treatment of tuberculosis. It was built on former Forest land, provided by the Duke of Portland, at Ratcher Hill.

147 In 1920 Berry Hill Hall was bought from the Hollins family and converted into a convalescent home for the local mining industry. Miners also benefited greatly from the Harlow Wood orthopaedic hospital, opened in 1929, just outside the Borough boundary. All the health institutions named above are now closed, most in the 1980s.

148 Bringing this chapter full-circle, here are some more examples of civic pride. In 1891, the town finally opted for Borough status, so the Improvement Commissioners were replaced by a Mayor and Council. The Royal Charter was delivered on 14 July, to a town replete with floral decorations, and a populace in party mood.

EAST WARD ELECTION.

VOTE

FOR

WALLIS & WHARMBY.

149 Borough status meant proper local elections (an electoral system devised for the Improvement Commissioners in 1874 had been, by modern standards, corrupt). Experienced councillor I.H. Wallis and novice J.J. Wharmby, who advertised himself as a Mansfield resident of some 18 years and 'no inconsiderable ratepayer', were Liberal candidates in the 1897 election.

150 Even in the first decades of the 20th century, the title 'Lord of the Manor' was treated with respect. The Duke and Duchess of Portland took a great interest in Mansfield, and the town returned their affection. This tin showing the Duke and Welbeck Abbey was made by Barringer's to celebrate the double anniversary year of 1914.

151 Some civic spectaculars had a very practical purpose, notably the Hospital Carnivals of the 1930s. Most famous of these was the 1932 Carnival, which had a theme of 'Old Mansfield'. It was the last major event in which the ailing A.S. Buxton took part, but just a hoot for 76-year-old former Mayor and Town Clerk John Harrop White, seen here.

152 Most pictures of royal visits concentrate on the scenes in the marketplace (see also the frontispiece). This photograph of the surprisingly narrow-looking Chesterfield Road at the time of the 1896 visit shows, however, that attention was also paid by the organisers to the whole route along which the visitors were to travel.

153 Mansfield had a positive love-affair with George and Mary. Vast crowds assembled in and around the marketplace for the celebrations of the Coronation in June 1911. Other photos show massed choirs of children, a decorated tram, and the crowd spilling up Albert Street, but here are the Mayor and Corporation returning to the Town Hall from church.

154 The King is almost invisible in this photo of the 1914 royal visit, waiting while the Mayor is presented to Queen Mary. Visits such as this set the 'meet the people' style we now expect from the Royal Family; after the formal reception, the King and Queen toured Barringer's factory and even ventured inside a miner's house at Forest Town.

The First World War

155 The First World War began much like any others in which Mansfield people had been involved. Troops paraded through the town on their way to foreign parts, just as in the Boer Wars a few years earlier, or indeed the Napoleonic Wars a century before. These cavalrymen are entering the town down Leeming Street in the winter of 1914-15.

fatigue · *A fair visitor*

bathing parade

R.M.P.

motor-orderly

Off duty

Fire piquet

The Transport Knut

REVEILLE

COMMISSIONED

CLIPSTONE CAMP. 1915

156 One major difference in 1915 was the creation of the vast Clipstone Camp just a few miles from the town. Thousands and thousands of soldiers (including my own great-uncle, who was not impressed by Clipstone) must have had brief glimpses of Mansfield on their way from purgatory to hell and, with luck, back to civilian life.

157 While the soldiers fought, those who stayed behind held parades and fairs to encourage the patriotic spirit and raise money for the war effort. Empire Day, the anniversary of Queen Victoria's birth on 24 May 1819, became an obvious morale-booster. This is the 1915 parade heading for a grand assembly on the Water Meadows.

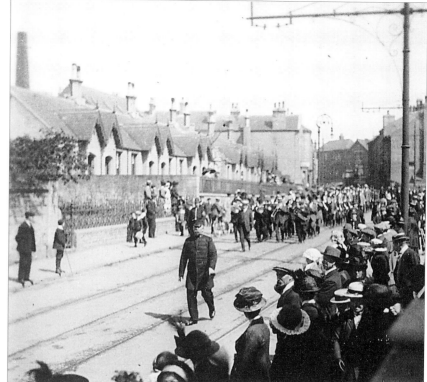

158 In the absence of radio, television, or even talking pictures, the art of public speaking on a cold and windy day was essential. Here, in the marketplace, the Duchess of Portland gives the opening speech for another savings effort, 'Broom Week', in 1918, while Mr Buxton valiantly tries to control his camera among the audience.

159 The patriotic spirit was further encouraged by the actions of the soldiers themselves. As early as March 1915, Wilfred Dolby Fuller, a professional soldier in the Grenadier Guards, performed a feat of almost cheeky heroism which won him the Victoria Cross. He was duly paraded through his home town in June, after the award was announced.

160 Here Fuller leaves his home on Skerry Hill, accompanied by the town worthies. The action which won him the nation's highest honour was the single-handed capture of 50 German soldiers, whom he found in a defensive trench and forced to accompany him by a messy demonstration of the power of his hand-grenades.

161 In 1916, declining health forced Fuller to leave the Army. Others were not given this option, and almost every week the newspapers included small portraits of those who had died. The *Chronicle* published special supplements, containing the 'Roll of Honour' (here from November 1914) plus a stirring story to encourage future warriors.

162 After the end of the war in 1918, the final accounting of the dead could begin. Factories, shops, schools, churches, all began the process of recording in stone the names of their men who would never return. This is the unveiling of the plaque at the Reed Mills, Bleak-Hills.

Aerial Atlas

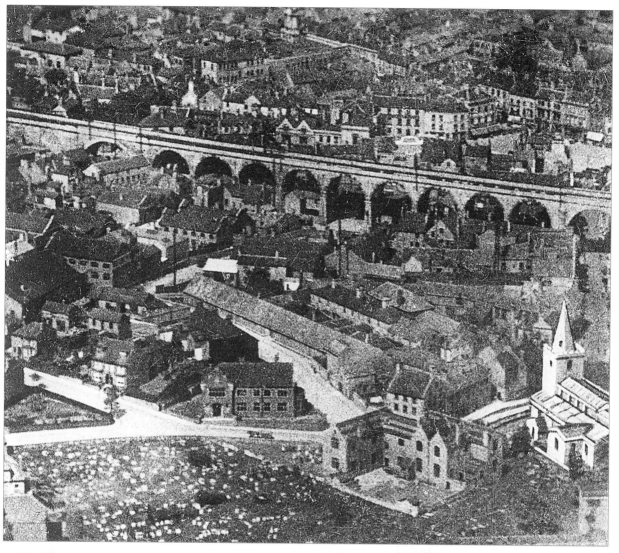

163 This is one of the first aerial photographs of Mansfield, taken in 1925 by Aerofilms, and published (with some retouching) as a postcard. Over the next few years, other photographs were taken for the Borough Council, and three of their original negatives form the basis of the aerial atlas which follows.

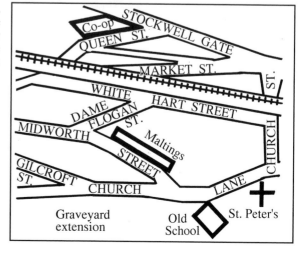

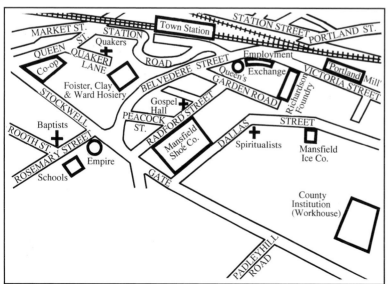

164 Photographed c.1931.

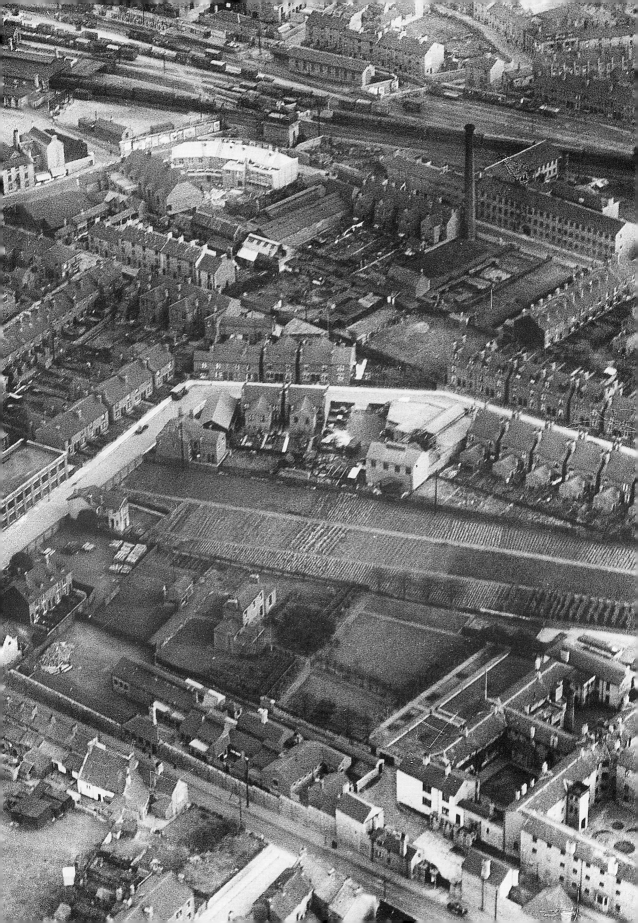

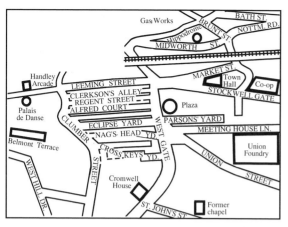

165   This photograph was taken c.1931.

166 This photograph was taken in 1929.

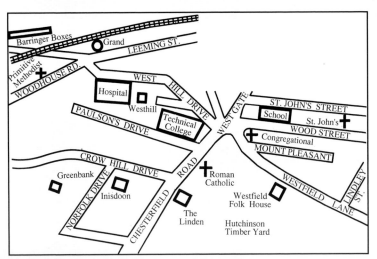

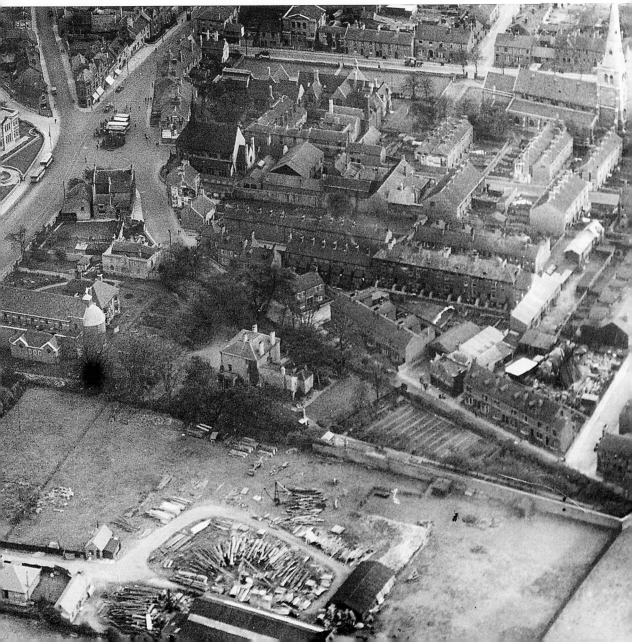

The Second World War

WOMEN'S EMERGENCY CORPS
AND
MANSFIELD RELIEF COMMITTEE

WORKROOM – White Hart St
MANSFIELD.

Toys made by MANSFIELD
GIRLS. Support a local
industry and make the
Children happy.

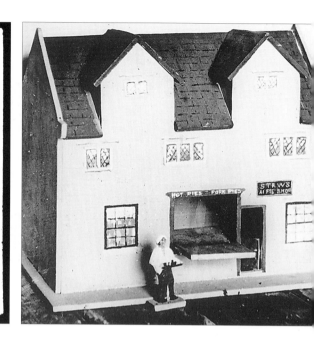

AIR RAID SHELTERS

Nearest shelters are
HANDLEY ARCADE
and
TOOTHILL ROAD

The Lecture will go
on for those
who care to remain

If you are interested
in the subject of this
lecture, why not read
more about it?

Books may be borrowed
free by all residents.

Your Public Library
has 34,000 books
to brighten blackout
evenings.

167 Use of fast bomber aircraft in the Second World War brought the conflict right into people's homes. Though some aspects were much as in 1914-18, such as the use of women to provide extra labour (making guns as well as toys, of course), community institutions had to work hard to encourage people to live a normal life.

168   As it happened, the bombers foolishly paid little attention to the Mansfield area (a great deal of the initial preparation for D-Day took place in Sherwood Forest). The library and museum on Leeming Street remained open, providing books, lectures and entertainment; so did the pubs, cinemas and other places of relief from the struggle.

169   The photographer who captured the parade during 'Back Your Boys Week' in June 1941 seems to have been perched nervously up a lamp-post. As in previous fund-raising efforts (see pictures 35 to 38) the major local firms put their best feet forward (or on this float, backward).

170 This more general view of the parade, heading down Albert Street towards Titchfield Park, shows that in this war, to a greater extent than previously, the nation was also Backing its Girls, who most notably dealt with the vast amounts of radio information from allied and enemy forces around the world, plus the new Radar systems.

Here are some of—

Mansfield Borough and Mansfield Woodhouse U.D. area are again joining in a great effort to lend money to the Government.

We have had our War Weapons and Warship Weeks. Now, it's "Wings for Victory" A big job has been given to us, but, WE CAN DO IT!

C. DAVEY,
Mayor of Mansfield & President of Campaign.

J. H. BROWN,
Chairman Mansfield Woodhouse U.D.C.

FRANK HARDY,
Chairman Mansfield Savings Association.
Mansfield & M Woodhouse War Finance Campaign

G. W. FARNSWORTH,
Chairman M Woodhouse Savings Association.

WINGS
FOR
VICTORY

19th to 26th JUNE, 1943

•

MANSFIELD
AND
MANSFIELD WOODHOUSE

𝔓rogramme   6ᴅ.

Mansfield's Heroes

171 As with the First World War, everybody was urged to make financial contributions, and there were campaigns for each branch of the armed forces. The big attraction in the 1943 'Wings for Victory' week was a remarkable exhibition at the Electricity Showrooms of photographs depicting local people who had joined the forces.

172 One successful fund-raising effort by the people of Mansfield resulted in the receipt by the council of a mass-produced commemorative plaque, and the christening of this Spitfire, in 1941. It spent most of its career as a reconnaissance plane, continuing in use after the war until it crashed in 1953.

173 By 1943 the aforementioned build-up to D-Day was in progress, and the Yanks had come to town. Here (discreetly unreported by the local press) the mayor helps to further international relations by presenting medals to two American soldiers in November of that year.

Presentation of Decorations 8th November, 1943, to two American soldiers, by Councillor C. Davey, Mayor

174 The film shortage seems to have precluded the use of cameras on VE Day, but a few weeks later a summer carnival was held to celebrate the victory. The librarian's photographer, from a vantage point on the top floor of the Town Hall, captured the vibrant atmosphere in the marketplace as the cavalcade passed through. The future was about to begin.

Bibliography

Ashton, Pauline *et al.*, *The Grace of God: Mansfield's Religious History* (2002)

Bradbury, David J., *Lost Mansfield* (1986)

Bradbury, David J., (comp.) *Mansfield in the News* (5 vols. 1990-1991)

Brettle, L., *A History of Queen Elizabeth's Grammar School for Boys, Mansfield* (1961)

Buxton, A.S., *Early Mansfield* (1987)

Buxton, A.S., *Historic Mansfield* (2 vols, 1972)

Gallon, Barbara *et al.*, *Nag's Head, King's Arms ...: Mansfield's Hostelry History* (1997)

Gamble, Tom, *Court in Time: Magistrates in Mansfield 1891-1978* (1999)

Groves, William H., *History of Mansfield* (1894)

Harrod, W., *History of Mansfield & its Environs* (1801)

Morley, Don *et al.*, *From Mills to Mines ...: Mansfield's Industrial History* (1996)

Old Mansfield Society, *Mansfield: The Last Century* (1991)

Old Mansfield Society, *Mansfield in World War II* (2003)

Orton, Leslie *et al.*, *Seats in All Parts: Mansfield's Stage & Screen History* (1998)

Retter, J. and Taylor, P., *Mansfield Town, the First 100 Years* (1997)

Savidge, Katherine and James, Rob, *Mansfield's Millennium 2000* (2000)

Index

Roman numerals refer to introductory text pages;
arabic numerals to illustrations and their captions.

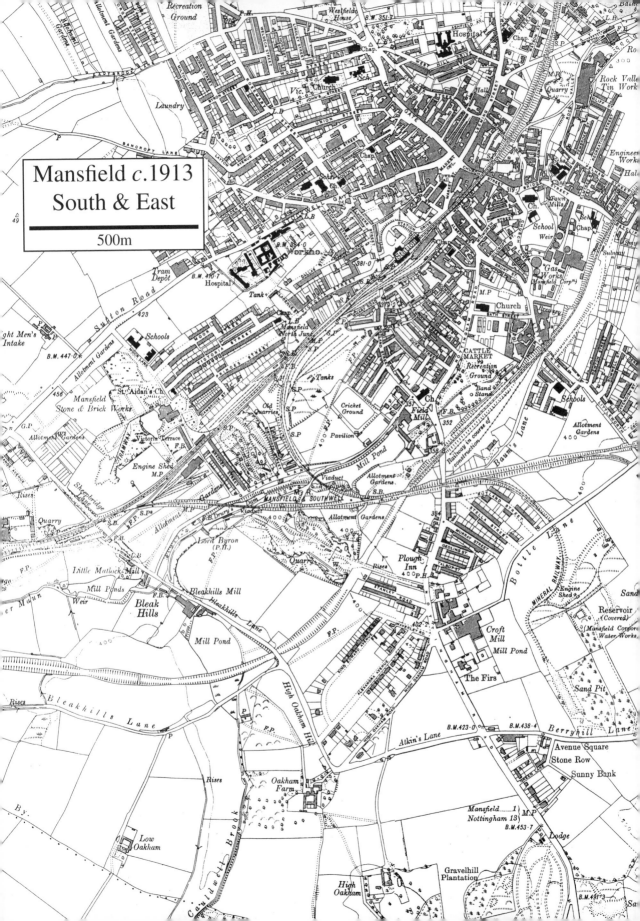

Mansfield *c.*1913
South & East

500m